THE
SYNAGOGUES
OF
LONDON

*The eternal lamp (Ner Tamid) in front of the Ark at the Spanish
and Portuguese Synagogue, Maida Vale*

The Synagogues of London

PAUL LINDSAY

With a Foreword by
Rev. Dr Isaac Levy

VALLENTINE MITCHELL

First published in 1993 in Great Britain by
VALLENTINE MITCHELL & CO LTD
Gainsborough House, Gainsborough Road,
London E11 1RS, England

and in the United States of America by
VALLENTINE MITCHELL
c/o International Specialized Book Services, Inc.
5602 N.E. Hassalo Street, Portland, Oregon 97213

Copyright © 1993 Paul Lindsay

British Library Cataloguing in Publication Data
Lindsay, Paul
  Synagogues of London
  I. Title
  726

    ISBN 0-85303-241-6 (hardback)
    ISBN 0-85303-258-0 (paperback)

Library of Congress Cataloging-in-Publication Data
Lindsay, Paul
    The synagogues of London/Paul Lindsay: with a
    foreword by Isaac Levy.
        p.   cm.
    Includes bibliographical references.
    ISBN 0-85303-241-6: ISBN 0-85303-258-0 (pbk.)
    1. Judaism – England – London – History.
    2. Synagogues – England – London – History.
    3. Jews – England – London – History.
    4. Synagogue architecture – England – London.
    5. Synagogues – England – London – Guidebooks.
    6. London (England) – Guidebooks.   I. Title.
    BM294.8.L56   1993
    296'.09421 – dc20
                                        92-21435
                                        CIP

Typeset by Vitaset, Paddock Wood, Kent
Printed in Great Britain by BPCC Wheatons Ltd, Exeter

Contents

List of Illustrations   8
Acknowledgements of Illustrations   10
Acknowledgements   11
Foreword by Rev. Dr Isaac Levy   13
Introduction   15

1. **The Jews of England**   17
   From the Norman Conquest to the Expulsion   17
   The Resettlement: 1650–56   20
   From Toleration to Emancipation   22
   Jews in London   27

2. **The Synagogue Movements**   29
   The Sephardim   29
   The United Synagogue   31
   The Federation of Synagogues   32
   The Union of Orthodox Hebrew Congregations   33
   The Reform Synagogues of Great Britain   34
   The Liberals: Union of Liberal and Progressive Synagogues 37

3. **The Synagogues of the City of London and the East End** 38
   Bevis Marks   38
   The Great   41
   The Hambro'   45
   Sandy's Row   47
   Machzike Hadath and the Spitalfields Great   49
   Fieldgate Street   51

The East London 53
Congregation of Jacob 55
The Wlodowa 55
Princelet Street 58
The Hackney 61
The Yavneh 61
Great Garden Street 65

4. **The West End Synagogues** 66
The Western 66
The Marble Arch 68
The Central 70
The West London 73
The New West End 76
The West Central 79
The Westminster 81
The West End Great 81
The Bayswater 84

5. **Synagogues in North London** 86
Stamford Hill 86
The New, Egerton Road 89
The North London Progressive 90

6. **Three Synagogues in West London** 92
Notting Hill 92
Hammersmith 96
Holland Park 96

7. **North-west London Synagogues** 99
The Spanish and Portuguese Synagogue, Maida Vale 99
The New London, Abbey Road 101
The St John's Wood, Grove End Road 101
Two Liberal Synagogues: 104
   The Liberal Jewish 104
   The Belsize Square 106
The Hampstead, Dennington Park Road 106
Two Synagogues in Hampstead: 110
   The Hampstead Adath 110
   The Hampstead Reform Jewish Community 110
Dollis Hill 111

8. **Golders Green and its Synagogues** 113
The Golders Green Synagogue, Dunstan Road 113

Beth Abraham, The Ridgeway   115
North-West Reform, Alyth Gardens   116
The Golders Green Beth Hamedrash Congregation   116

9. Synagogue Architecture in London   118

Appendix 1: The Architects   123
Appendix 2: Map of the East End (showing principal synagogues)   124
           Map of the West End (showing principal synagogues)   126
Appendix 3: Directory of Synagogues in Greater London   129

Glossary   133
Bibliography   135

List of Illustrations

The eternal lamp (Ner Tamid) in front of the Ark at the Spanish
    and Portuguese Synagogue, Maida Vale   frontispiece

Menasseh Ben Israel   20
Plaque on the Cunard building in Creechurch Lane   22
The Royal Exchange, 1788   23
Jewish old-clothes man, 1820   24
Completing the writing of the Torah, Mill Hill Synagogue   28
Bevis Marks, City of London   30
The Chief Rabbi, Hermann Adler, 1904   31
Chasidim binding a new Scroll   35
Ner Tamid at Bevis Marks   39
Haham D. Nieto; Sir Moses Montefiore   40
Daniel Mendoza   41
The Great Synagogue, 1809   42
The Great Synagogue at Duke's Place, 1722   43
Mrs Judith Levy: 'the Queen of Richmond Green'   44
The Hambro', Fenchurch Street (1725–1893)   46
Sandy's Row, Spitalfields   48
The Spitalfields Great Synagogue, Brick Lane   50
The new Machzikei Hadath, Golders Green   51
Fieldgate Synagogue, Stepney, exterior and interior   52
Reverend Joseph F. Stern   53
East London Synagogue, Stepney Green   54
Congregation of Jacob, Commercial Road   56
The Wlodowa Synagogue, Cheshire Street   57
Interior of the Wlodowa Synagogue   58

Princelet Street Synagogue   59
The Hackney Synagogue   60
The Yavneh   62
The Yavneh (interior)   63
Great Garden Street Synagogue   64
A stained-glass window at the Western Synagogue   67
Marble Arch Synagogue: inside the Ark   69
Consecration of the new Central Synagogue, 1870   70
The Central Synagogue, 1870; the Marriage of Mr Leopold
    de Rothschild and Mademoiselle Marie Perugia in the
    Central Synagogue   71
The New Central Synagogue, 1958   72
The West London Synagogue   74
West London Synagogue: Ordination Service of Rabbis   75
The New West End Synagogue (interior)   77
The New West End Synagogue (exterior)   78
Lily Montagu, Minister of the West Central Synagogue   79
The Westminster Synagogue: the barrel-vaulted ceiling   80
The West End Great Synagogue, Dean Street   82
Bayswater Synagogue (interior)   83
The New Synagogue, Stamford Hill   88
Entrance to synagogue in Leadenhall Street, 1811   90
North London Progressive Synagogue   91
Notting Hill Synagogue   93
Hammersmith Synagogue, Brook Green   94
Ritual silver at Hammersmith Synagogue   95
The Spanish and Portuguese Synagogue, Holland Park   97
The Spanish and Portuguese Synagogue, Maida Vale   100
The New London Synagogue, Abbey Road   102
The St John's Wood Synagogue   103
The Ark of the former Liberal Jewish Synagogue   105
The Hampstead Synagogue   107
The octagonal domed interior at Hampstead Synagogue   109
Dollis Hill Synagogue   111
The Golders Green Synagogue   114
Beth Abraham Synagogue, Golders Green   115
Ground plan of the United Synagogue standard interior   119

Acknowledgements of Illustrations

Grateful acknowledgement is made to the following for permission to reproduce illustrations:

John Brandenburger for The Eternal Lamp at the Lauderdale Road Synagogue; Site of first synagogue in Creechurch Lane; Bevis Marks Synagogue; Sandy's Row Synagogue; Fieldgate Street Synagogue, E1; East London Synagogue, Stepney Green; Wlodowa Synagogue; Congregation of Jacob; The Hackney Synagogue; The Yavneh; The Western Synagogue; The new Central Synagogue (interior); West London Synagogue; New West End Synagogue (Bayswater); Marble Arch Synagogue – inside the Ark; The Westminster Synagogue (entrance hall at Kent House); The West End Great; The New, Egerton Road, N16; North London Progressive Synagogue, Stamford Hill; The Hammersmith Synagogue, Brook Green; The Spanish and Portuguese Synagogue, Holland Park; Notting Hill Synagogue; The Spanish and Portuguese Synagogue, Lauderdale Road; The New London Synagogue, Abbey Road; St John's Wood Synagogue, Grove End Road; Ark of the Liberal Jewish Synagogue; The Hampstead Synagogue, Dennington Park Road; Dollis Hill Synagogue.

Stuart Eames for the Golders Green Synagogue; the Beth Abraham Synagogue, NW11; The Hampstead Synagogue (cover photograph).

Peter Fisher for Mill Hill Synagogue; The new Machzikei Hadath, Golders Green; West London Synagogue – Ordination Service of Rabbis.

Sidney Harris for Chasidim binding a new scroll (1986).

Alfred Rubens, *History of Jewish Costume* for Menasseh Ben Israel: etching by Rembrandt; The Chief Rabbi, Herman Adler, 1904; The Royal Exchange, 1788; 'Old clothes to sell'; Haham D. Nieto; Sir Moses Montefiore and Daniel Mendoza.

Cecil Roth, *History of the Great Synagogue* for the Great Synagogue (reprinted from J.R. Ackermann, *The Microcosm of London*); for Mrs Judith Levy; and for the Hambro' Synagogue, Fenchurch Street.

The Jewish Chronicle for The Spitalfields Great Synagogue; The Bayswater (Interior).

Tower Hamlets Local Library for Rev. Joseph F. Stern.

The London Museum of Jewish Life for Princelet Street Synagogue.

The *Graphic Magazine* (16 April 1870) for Consecration of the Central Synagogue.

The *European Magazine* for Entrance to the New Synagogue, Leadenhall Street.

Acknowledgements

I wish to express my gratitude to those friends who helped to get the project started and completed. In particular, acknowledgement is made to Shirley Kleiman who gave so generously of her time and energy to background fact-finding and interviewing synagogue officials. Her research was invaluable.

I acknowledge the help given by Reggie Grant who read the manuscript and, of course, I thank John Brandenburger for the photographs which contributed so much to the book.

My special thanks to Eileen Truran who typed my notes – no easy task – and patiently re-typed the text.

My wife, Diana, kept the project going and it would never have been finished without her encouragement and support.

Paul Lindsay
Highgate, March 1991

Foreword

The synagogue as a place of worship, a house of study and a social centre is the oldest Jewish communal institution. Although it is generally accepted that it originated in the Babylonian exile, there is every reason to believe that centres of worship existed long before the destruction of the first Temple. It was, however, during the second Temple period that synagogues proliferated throughout Palestine and the Diaspora, and ever since the synagogue has served as the dynamic centre for Jewish communal activity.

The very names by which it is known are indicative of its function. The word synagogue is of Greek origin. Its Hebrew equivalent, *beth ha knesset* – the 'House of Assembly' – recalls that it represents a congregational meeting-place. The name *shul*, so often used in common parlance, is a derivative of the German *Schule* (school), which points to the educational role that it played, for it was here that both elementary and adult education was conducted. The fact that many synagogues bear the title *kehilla kedoshah* ('Holy Congregation') indicates that congregational life was established and maintained through the synagogue's centrality.

The siting of synagogues reflects the history of congregations and the mobility of the community. Wherever Jews settled priority was given to the establishment of a place of worship. This might take the form of a modest building or a *shtiebl*, a room, where worshippers gathered for daily, Sabbath and Festival services. In time this assumed the form of a more elaborate structure built in accordance with a distinctive architectural design dependent on the affluence of those concerned. This upward mobility of the community frequently witnessed a decline in the use of an earlier building as worshippers moved away from former centres of settlement to take up residence in more salubrious districts in the Metropolis or its suburbs. Thus the synagogue plays an important function in recording the life of the community.

Paul Lindsay's pioneering work in reviving memories of some of those earlier synagogues is a distinct contribution to Anglo-Jewish history. This book will serve as a valuable *vade mecum* for the tourist who visits London and seeks information on the religious life of the community. It will also help to resurrect memories of bygone days when our Ashkenazi forebears from Eastern Europe and our Sephardi ancestors from the Netherlands settled in the East End of London, there to create a vibrant Jewish community.

There may be some who are tempted to say *sic transit gloria* and relegate the ancient edifices to the limbo of forgetfulness, but those who cherish respect for the past will share the enthusiasm of Paul Lindsay in the revival of historic memory.

Rev. Dr I. Levy

Introduction

No other city in Europe has a greater collection of large and small synagogues than London. More than 150 houses of worship are in use and are a close reflection of the history of the Jews of London. Many old synagogues are dying and their buildings are in danger of being demolished or transformed to other uses. Some of these are important in the history of the Anglo-Jewish community and are recorded in these pages. New synagogues are being built or reconstructed to fit the changed circumstances of our time. Above all, the synagogues described reflect the diversity of the Anglo-Jewish community. Judaism is not a monolithic religion and the synagogues of London show the whole range of 'sects' and Movements from the most Orthodox *shtiebl* to the most Progressive or Reform congregations.

Not all the synagogues included are treasures of architecture but all are worth recording, as their history is an integral part of the history of the Jews of London. In some cases, remarkable men and women have been associated with the synagogues and are important to the history of the Anglo-Jewish community. Some of the buildings contain valuable relics or like Bevis Marks in the City of London are splendid temples – living reminders and witnesses to the long story of the Jews in London.

London is, of course, a vast city, and its synagogues are scattered far and wide over the sprawling conurbation. This is not a comprehensive guide and no attempt has been made to include every synagogue in every district from Stanmore in the north-west to Ilford in the eastern suburbs. The selection has been made partly on the basis of history, partly architectural interest and partly to show examples of the variety of synagogue movements. The synagogues of London began in the City of London and later developed in the East End. They have spread north, south, west and east as the population of Jewish London has changed and moved. This selective guide is offered to those who want to know more about a neglected aspect of London and its Jewish citizens.

I

The Jews of England

From the Norman Conquest to the Expulsion

Jews are not newcomers to Britain. Jewish soldiers may have come to this country with Julius Caesar and there are stories of early Jewish settlers in Cornwall. But the first recorded settlement of Jews in London and in other English towns took place early in the reign of William the Conqueror, Duke of Normandy. The king encouraged the Jews of Normandy to follow him for very practical reasons: he needed the money in coin that they brought with them. At first Jews followed their Norman lord in the hope of greater economic opportunities and a freer life. Within a generation, they were impelled by the need to escape the massacres of the Jews in Rouen in the last decade of the eleventh century.

Under the relatively benign rule of the Norman kings, William I, William Rufus and Henry I, Jews enjoyed protection within the law and some rights and privileges. Not only were they useful in supplying the royal treasury, but it was expedient to make use of them – and blame them – for financial dealing forbidden to Christians by the Church. In return for their services, a Charter was granted by Henry I, giving his Jewish subjects freedom of movement in the country at large, and their goods, like those of the king himself, were excused all tolls and customs. They were permitted to live wherever they wished, and were entitled to claim redress if molested and to hold land in pledge until redeemed. Moreover, Jews were granted the right to be tried by their peers and to be sworn on the Pentateuch. Most remarkable of all, considering the oppressive times to come, the oath of a Jew was considered valid against the oaths of twelve Christians.

In the two centuries before the expulsion, Jews were widely dispersed over England and Wales. After London, Oxford and Cambridge, Norwich had the largest number of Jewish inhabitants. Isaac of Norwich, a great merchant, was one of the richest men in England. His good fortune ended in 1210 when he was imprisoned with other Jews by King John, who also seized his London house and later presented it to the Earl of Derby.

A Jewish community in Oxford is recorded as early as the year 1075, and a few years later there are references to their school and a synagogue. Stamford was such an important centre that the Church authorities sent monks there (in 1109) to preach to the people against Judaism and the influence of Jews. The first reliable reference to Jews in London is in the year 1115 and the first settlement was in the Ward of Haco in Broad Street.[1] The earliest synagogues were within the City of London: both St. Stephen's and St. Mary, Colechurch, were once synagogues until they were confiscated and handed over to the Church. The building which became St. Anthony's Hospital (a City of London bank now occupies the site) was once used as a synagogue. The favourable years for the Jews in England in the early part of the reign of Henry I had encouraged them to embark on the construction of a 'magnificent'[2] house of worship, probably to replace other humbler houses of prayer already used in the City. When the building was completed it aroused great envy and hostility and the king was petitioned for its confiscation. The 'prayer' was granted in 1232 and the fine new building together with its outbuildings was consecrated to the Virgin and given to the Brethren of St. Anthony of Vienna, from which the name St. Anthony's Hospital is derived.

Old Jewry, the street in the City, had a place of worship on its north-east corner which was also confiscated and granted to the Order of the Sackcloth Friars, who had complained about the 'howling of the Jews at prayer'.[3] This was but one of a number of synagogues, many in private houses, that were subjected to confiscation and suppression from the year 1232 until the Expulsion in 1290.

If life for the Jews under the early Norman kings had been protected and England seemed 'an Island of Refuge', it was dangerously dependent on the goodwill of the monarch. After the death of Henry I in 1135, civil war broke out and popular discontent turned into violent demonstrations against Jewry. In fact, the 'honeymoon period' had already ended in the last few years of Henry's reign. As the Jews prospered, feelings of envy and hatred were easily aroused against these people who lived apart and were alien in religion, in race and in appearance. But the first significant attack on the rights of the Jews did not come from the common people, nor from the Church, nor from the landed gentry, but from the king himself. As a result of the death of a sick man who had been treated by a Jewish doctor, the king fined the Jews of London the huge sum of two thousand pounds – its modern equivalent would be about one million.

Worse accusations and outrages were to come. In the unsettled times in the reign of Stephen (1135–54) the so-called 'Blood Libel' was first heard in England; later it became infamous on the Continent. William of Norwich, a 12-year-old apprentice, was found dead in a wood near the city on the day before Good Friday, 1144. His death was described as a 'ritual murder' to mock the Crucifixion before the Jewish Feast of the Passover. The evidence could hardly have been convincing, as even the Sheriff of Norwich would not allow the Jews to appear in the Bishop's Court to answer the charge and instead took them under his own protection. In spite of the Sheriff, many Norwich Jews were killed and many more fled from the town. William of Norwich was later canonised as a Holy Martyr. The Blood Libel was to be heard against the Jews of Gloucester in 1168 and again in London and in other English towns in the years to follow.

The reign of Richard I proved to be a tragic period of bloodshed and persecution for the small communities of Jews in England. The king himself was not ill-disposed towards his Jewish subjects, but his absence from his realm in the Crusades left the way open to some of the worst outbreaks of anti-Semitism ever recorded in English history. Even on the very day of his coronation, Jews were attacked and killed. Many contemporary accounts, though different, agree that a deputation of leading Jews tried to present the new king with gifts from a number of communities in various parts of the kingdom. They were not allowed into Westminster Hall but mingled with the crowd at the gates.

It is not known what sparked off the violence, but Jews and women had been officially barred from attending the coronation ceremony – 'because of the magic arts which Jews and some women notoriously exercise at Royal coronations'. Anti-Jewish rabble-rousers seem to have taken advantage of the proclamation as a licence to attack the deputation of Jews bearing rich gifts. The crowd was quickly aroused, and a riot broke out in which several members of the deputation were beaten and some killed. The violence was not confined to Westminster; wild rumours that the new king had decreed that all Jews were to be destroyed were heard in the streets of the City. Jewish homes in the Jewry were set on fire. Some Jews took refuge in the Tower of London; others were taken into the homes of their Christian neighbours. Thirty Jews were killed, among them an eminent Rabbi, Jacob of Orleans, who had recently arrived from the Continent.

The young king, while at the banquet following his coronation, heard of the outbreak and sent officials to calm the mobs. Later several of the ringleaders were arrested and hanged, but the riots continued for more than 24 hours. The king gave orders that the Jews were to be left in peace. But the royal proclamation was of little effect once Richard crossed to the Continent to gather forces for the Crusades.

The worst episode in Anglo-Jewish history took place a year after Richard came to the throne. While the king was abroad pursuing the 'enemies of the Cross', the way was left open for an anti-Jewish 'crusade' in England. It began in Lynn in Norfolk, where a small Jewish settlement was all but wiped out, and culminated in the massacre at York in 1190. The attack on the Jews of York began with the plunder of the house of a wealthy Jew named Benedict, who had died on his return journey to his home. Taking advantage of his absence, a mob attacked and killed Benedict's widow and children and destroyed the house. The rest of the Jewish community were so alarmed by the violence that they took refuge in York Castle. For the besieged Jews there seemed only the terrible choice between self-destruction and being slain by a mob among whom was a monk urging them to 'destroy the enemies of Christ'.[4]

With them in the tower of the castle was their Rabbi, Yomtob of Joigny, who urged his fellow Jews to remember and emulate their ancestors at Masada. In fact, most of the community did take their own lives. The remainder, who could not kill their wives and children and themselves, were promised mercy if they would become Christians. As these few families emerged from the castle, they were seized and slaughtered. Not one person survived of an established community of some fifteen hundred Jews.

During the hundred years before the Expulsion there were periods of relative calm when the Jews of England were allowed to prosper and even to regain some of their legal and civil rights. Increasingly, however, the situation of the Jews worsened, and England no longer seemed a place of refuge from persecution on the Continent. At best, when the king needed 'his Jews' to prevent a serious loss of revenue, liberal treatment and protection became the order of the day. King John in the early part of his reign, at the beginning of the thirteenth century, acted generously and in an enlightened way towards the Jews; in 1201 he drew up a remarkable Charter which was granted to the Jews of England and Normandy.

All the rights and privileges granted by William II and Henry I were restored – at a price, four thousand marks, payable by the Jewish community as a whole in half-yearly instalments. At about the same time the 'Exchequer of the Jews' – largely a register of Jewish property, assets and debts – was set up, its primary function being to ensure a steady flow of money and property from Jewish ownership into the royal treasury.

The accession to the throne of the boy-king Henry III brought some relief to the Jews from the squeezing, impoverishment and sporadic cruelty of the reign of John. The government, in the hands of the Earl of Pembroke who acted as Regent, restored some rights to the Jews. One of the Regent's first acts was to order the immediate release of all Jews in prison, no matter what the charges against them. In the following year the sheriffs were commanded to choose 24 burgesses for every town in which Jews lived and to protect them against ill-treatment by crusaders. The respite did not last; as the new regime showed sympathy for the Jews so the Church became more hostile. Stephen Langton, Archbishop of Canterbury, at a synod in Oxford in 1222 demanded penalties on the Jews: 'Let them not be permitted to build any more synagogues, but be looked upon as debtors to the churches of the parishes wherein they reside . . . to prevent likewise the mixture of Jewish men and women with Christians, we charge that the Jews wear a linen cloth of a different colour from their own clothes before their breast' – an ominous demand which at that time was not approved by the king. The yellow badge was introduced by Pope Innocent III at the Lateran Council of 1215 to discourage social relations between Christians and Jews. In England, it took the form of the two tablets of the Ten Commandments.

As the Jews became less necessary to the English monarchs, so they proved less willing to protect their Jewish subjects from attacks by the landed gentry, the hostility of the Church or the violence of the town mob. The Jews repeatedly pleaded with Henry III for permission to leave England with their families and their property. The king always refused. The time had not yet come when they were no longer of any use as moneylenders to the Crown and contributors to the Treasury.

The last phase for the Jews in medieval England came in the reign of Edward I (1272–1307). During the later years of the thirteenth century foreign bankers and merchants had made other sources of capital available, and with the beginnings of a moneyed English merchant class, the Jews became dispensable. Edward was not only more religious than his father but more inclined to carry out the Church of Rome's strict policy against usury. With his active approval, Parliament enacted the Statute de Judaismo in 1275 which not only forbade usury but prevented the recovery of interest due. The effect of the Statute was the drastic impoverishment of the Jews, who had been excluded for 200 years from any occupation other than financial by successive kings and their governments. Their means of earning their living having been destroyed, many Jews became desperate and some, no doubt, resorted to tampering with the coinage. The clipping of coins was regarded as a grave offence, and when the king decided to reform the currency in 1278, he decided to make an example of the Jews as the principal threat to the maintenance of the coin of the realm. All the Jews in the country were arrested and imprisoned and their homes were searched. At the trials not only Jews but a larger number of Christians were found guilty, yet only three non-Jews were sentenced to death. In London alone, 293 Jews were hanged for the same offence.

The persecution went on. In 1279, it was proclaimed that any Jew found guilty of blaspheming Christian doctrine would be severely punished. A Jew was burnt for this offence at Norwich. In the last decade before the Expulsion, the whole of Anglo-Jewry was once again imprisoned and only released on payment of a ransom of twelve thousand pounds of silver. In 1282, although the chief synagogues had already been seized and closed in the reign of Henry III, the remaining smaller houses of worship were suppressed. The policy of the Church became increasingly hostile and the king was fully prepared to carry out its condemnation of 'the accursed and perfidious Jews'. Finally, on 18 July 1290, Edward carried out the wishes of his Parliament and ordered the Jews to leave England by 1 November, All Saints' Day.

Thus about 16,000 Jews from London and 16 other towns left England mostly for Normandy, Flanders and parts of Germany. The king took measures to ensure that the departing Jews were not robbed or harmed. Unhappily, the king's wishes were not heeded; not only were they insulted and attacked on their last journey from this country but many were shipwrecked and drowned on the crossing to the Continent. A few who preferred conversion to Christianity were permitted to remain, but effectively England had rid itself of the Jews. There was to be no overt Jewish settlement nor a Jewish community in England for nearly 400 years.

The Resettlement: 1650–56

In spite of the Expulsion, there was probably no period when Jews were totally excluded from this country. Crypto-Jews, called by the Spanish name Marranos, managed to enter England under the guise of Protestant refugees fleeing from persecution by the Catholic authorities in Spain. A small number of Marranos managed to survive in England until the middle of the sixteenth century when the short but brutal reign of Mary (1553–58) brought the persecution of the Inquisition into England. During those five years, even the few Crypto-Jews had to leave England in fear of their lives.

Unlike her sister Mary, Elizabeth I seemed favourably disposed to Jews. The appointment of Roderigo Lopez, a Portuguese Jew, as her chief physician is evidence of a new attitude to Jews as well as a tribute to the knowledge and skill of a man who had been brought to England as a prisoner by Sir Francis Drake. Unhappily, as a result of a Court intrigue, he was accused of plotting against the Queen's life and was executed in 1594. There were other eminent Jewish doctors in Elizabethan England: a certain Jacob was admitted to the College of Physicians in 1585 at the express wish of the Queen and later sent by her to attend to the Czar of Russia. Undoubtedly, an awareness was developing of Jews in literature and in history in the England of the late sixteenth and seventeenth centuries. The Reformation had aroused a new interest in the Old Testament and in the People of the Book. Not only were there leading roles in Marlowe's *The Jew of Malta*, Thomas Dekker's *The Jew of Venice*, and, of course, Shylock in Shakespeare's *Merchant of Venice* but also there were many references to Jewish customs and to Jews in many other contemporary dramas. During Elizabeth's reign there was a small but significant influx of individual Jewish merchants and scholars from Spain and Portugal who for a time enjoyed prosperity and some tacit acceptance.

But it was the Civil War in the mid-seventeenth century and the Commonwealth under Cromwell that made possible the Resettlement of Jews in England. In the three centuries since the Expulsion England had been profoundly changed from a backwater of Europe into an international trading nation and one of the centres of European commerce. By the time of the Commonwealth, the climate of religious opinion had changed greatly in favour of toleration of Non-conformists, heretics and even of Jews. The Puritans who ruled England were, in fact, committed to the principles of tolerance and were deeply influenced by their reading of the Hebrew Scriptures. Some Puritans welcomed the prospect of closer contact with the descendants of the Israelites, God's Chosen People. The time was ripe in many ways for the readmission of the Jews.

Rabbi Menasseh Ben Israel, a leading member of the Jewish community in Amsterdam, played an important part in persuading the leaders of the Commonwealth to consider the Resettlement. Having achieved renown in both Christian and Jewish academic circles by presenting Judaism in a favourable light to the non-Jewish mind, his pamphlet on the discovery of the Ten Lost Tribes of

Menasseh Ben Israel. Etching by Rembrandt

Israel attracted great attention in England. The Rabbi shrewdly dedicated the pamphlet (called 'The Hope of Israel') to the English Parliament. The Puritans were flattered by the learned Rabbi's attention and fascinated by his claim in the pamphlet that the Messianic age was imminent. Rabbi Ben Israel had argued that according to Biblical prophecy the discovery of Jews in South America showed that the scattering of the Jews to all parts of the earth was nearing completion and thus heralding the Millennium. Re-admission of the Jews into England would complete the Diaspora; thus any country without Jews, Menasseh claimed, would delay the Second Coming, and England was almost the only country in the civilised world closed to the Children of Israel.

It is unlikely that the hard-headed Oliver Cromwell was much influenced by these Messianic arguments. He was, however, known to be disposed towards the abolition of the Edict of Expulsion of 1290, largely for economic reasons. The Lord Protector was fully aware of the prosperity of other European centres of trade, particularly Amsterdam, where Jews were allowed to use their commercial skills and exploit their international connections with other Jewish merchants. Cromwell saw the advantages that could result from re-admitting the Jews and seemed prepared to open the way to negotiations on their behalf. Although his Council of State considered the question, they never came to a clear decision in favour of re-admission. No doubt they were influenced by the outspoken opposition to the admission of the Jews in the numerous pamphlets published at the time. War broke out with Holland in 1653, and other pressing matters pushed 'the Jewish question' into the background. Menasseh Ben Israel was not able to press the matter owing to the difficulty of travelling between the warring countries and the official Mission set up to consider the re-admission of the Jews could not function.

Yet only three years later when England found itself also at war with Spain, the status of the Jews became an issue again. The war with Spain had one immediate consequence: a Proclamation by the Privy Council declared that all property of Spaniards in England was 'lawful prize'. The Marranos, who had not been whole-heartedly in favour of Menasseh's campaign on their behalf for fear of the attention it drew to them, now found themselves in a critical position. An informer had brought about the seizure of the property of Antonio Rodriquez Robles, a wealthy Marrano merchant. The rest of the Marranos, many of Spanish nationality, realised that they had no choice but to come out into the open as Jews and claim the protection of the Common-wealth. In fact, they did more and petitioned for official permission to worship freely and to acquire their own communal burial ground. At the same time a petition addressed by Robles to Cromwell pleaded for 'the proverbial hospitality of England' for himself, for his family and all other Jews persecuted by the Spanish Inquisition. This petition was supported by affidavits and signed by all the leading Marranos living at that time in London. The Council of State, after a little hesitation (they passed the responsibility to the Admir-alty Commissioners), decided to take a favourable view of Robles' claim and his property was restored to him. Although the government had not resolved the ambiguous status of the Jews in England, the position of the Marranos had been made more secure. Rights of residence and trade began to be granted, and soon afterwards Cromwell himself directed the City of London to place 'no impediments in the way of the Jews'. For their part the Jews had to agree not to encourage 'an indiscriminate immigration, not to obtrude their worship and ceremonies in public . . . and to make no converts'. Henceforth, significantly, the maintenance of a synagogue was permitted and the right to acquire a cemetery.

It was not what Menasseh Ben Israel had striven for, and he was bitterly disappointed by the outcome. For years he had worked for England to be open to Jewish refugees from persecution in many parts of Europe. The compromise that tacitly allowed the Marranos to remain unmolested in England seemed to him a betrayal of the interests of European Jewry. All that had been achieved was a recognition by the Commonwealth of the 'status quo'. Nevertheless, the Jewish presence in England became legitimate and an Anglo-Jewish community could exist unobtrusively within a reasonably secure framework. The fact that no law had been passed was disappointing but perhaps a blessing in those uncertain times. Laws can be repealed by a change in Parliament and a new government could have revoked a declaration in favour of Jewish resettlement. The absence of such laws and the ambiguity of the position of the Jews may have helped the small community in the upheavals that followed the death of Cromwell and the end of the Commonwealth.

By the time the monarchy was restored in 1660, the Jewish community in London is estimated to have been about 35 families. The names were, of course, predominantly Spanish and Portuguese: Pereiras, D'Oliveiras, Rodrigues and Henriques among others. At the time of the 'Glorious Revolution' (1688) that

Plaque on the Cunard building in Creechurch Lane in the City of London marking the site of the first synagogue established after the re-admission of the Jews to England

brought William and Mary to the throne, there were more than 100 Jewish families in London with two synagogues: one for the Sephardim in Creechurch Lane in the city, and the other for the few Ashkenazi families in St Helen's, Bishopsgate. The synagogue in Creechurch Lane had been in existence for some time but its services had been conducted with secrecy. During the relaxed atmosphere of Restoration England, the existence of this synagogue became public knowledge and services were held more and more openly. It even became a fashionable place to visit, as we can see from Samuel Pepys' Diary.[5] The synagogue was little more than the upper part of a house using two rooms, the larger for the men and the smaller for the women. As was the custom in Spain and Portugal, the two rooms were separated by a partition with a long, narrow, lattice window.

Before the end of the seventeenth century, the community had grown and prospered and had decided to build a large new synagogue. Thus, the first 'purpose-built' synagogue in England was planned in 1695 and consecrated in the year 1701 in Bevis Marks, where it still stands.

From Toleration to Emancipation

In the two centuries from 1700 to 1900 England became once again an 'Island of Refuge', a country which enabled Jews to live in relative freedom and with protection from the law. For some it offered increasing opportunities to practise honourable professions and to become wealthy and respectable. During the eighteenth century, Jews were tolerated but suffered many legal handicaps. A Jew could not be accepted as a freeman of the City of London and thus could not participate in the City's retail trade and was excluded from some of the Chartered trading companies. Many Jews at that time were still aliens and therefore subject to handicaps that would not have applied if they had been naturalised. Naturalisation, however, was a difficult and expensive business and involved taking the sacrament. There were enlightened Members of Parliament, especially in the Lords, and in 1753 a Bill was passed, despite opposition in the Commons, removing the necessity of Jews to take the sacrament. The resulting anti-Semitic outburst was extraordinary (the total number of Jews in England was less than 8,000). The 'Jew Bill', as it was called, provoked chanting in the streets of London: 'No Jews, no wooden shoes' and Parliamentary supporters, even Bishops who had voted for the Bill in the Lords, were attacked. The government lost its political nerve, and the Bill was repealed.

Compared with the position of Jews in Central and Eastern Europe, however, England seemed a haven of freedom and opportunity. Persecution in Europe caused a constant flow of poverty-stricken refugees who were helped to Amsterdam and then passed on to London where they were encouraged to keep going to other places in the provinces or the Colonies. Although the number of Jews escaping from Prussia and Poland was nothing like the influx a century later, the older more settled Ashkenazi families felt unable to cope with the problems of these impoverished Jewish newcomers. In 1771, the Great Synagogue refused relief to the refugees on the grounds that 'they had left their country without good cause'!

The Anglo-Jewish community had been predomin-antly Sephardic during the Resettlement period, but increasingly they were outnumbered by the growth of the Ashkenazi community. An increasing proportion of the Sephardim were of English birth, and their freedom to move into new professions speeded up the process of assimilation and Anglicisation. Intermarriage and dispersal to other parts of England all combined to bring about the relative decline of the Sephardim. The establishment of Ashkenazi synagogues in London in the eighteenth century clearly shows the changing character of the Anglo-Jewish population.

The first Ashkenazi synagogue had been created in Broad Court, a short distance from Creechurch Lane, in 1690 by Jews of German and Polish origin. By 1720 they had outgrown their accommodation – a private house – and with the money provided by Moses Hart, a wealthy member of the congregation, a new site was

The Royal Exchange (1788)
A figure in a long cloak is seen on the right. His beard and appearance identify him as a foreign-born Ashkenazi Jew

acquired in Duke's Place, Aldgate. Thus in 1722, the Great Synagogue was built and became the leading synagogue of the Ashkenazi community in England. The Ashkenazim established its second synagogue, the Hambro' in 1726 soon after the opening of the Great. In fact, the Hambro' which derives its name from the Hamburg congregations on whose customs and practices it was based, was the result of disputes which caused a split and a breakaway from the congregation centred on the Great Synagogue.

The third Ashkenazi synagogue to be established in the Georgian period was the New in Leadenhall Street at the Bricklayers' Hall. This was another breakaway congregation from the Great Synagogue and for many years relations between the New Synagogue and the parent congregations were strained. However, as all three of the Ashkenazi congregations continued to flourish, in time they joined amicably together to form the nucleus of the United Synagogue.

The Anglo-Jewish elite, whether Sephardic or Ashkenazi, wanted to look and live like English gentlemen and ladies. They wanted to be indistinguishable from upper-class Christians without having to give up their Jewish faith. Merchant bankers, stockbrokers, jewellers and general merchants – all longed to feel at home in England. The same aims pervaded the shopkeepers and wholesalers just below them on the social and economic ladder. The long beards and distinctive clothes of the European Jew were abandoned in favour of clean-shaven features and fashionable clothes. Their wives were equally eager to be à la mode in dress and in hairstyle. They abandoned the *sheitel** (flouting the tradition that their own hair should not be seen) and ignored the rules governing modesty in dress.

The majority of the Jews in London were not wealthy bankers but poor hawkers and street traders. Many Sephardim were poor refugees fleeing the renewed activities of the Inquisition in the Iberian Peninsula. Moreover, in the latter part of the eighteenth century there was a flow of Sephardim from the impoverished communities of Turkey, Gibraltar and North Africa. In spite of the image of the Anglo-Sephardic Jew as a rich merchant banker and the Ashkenazi as a *schnorrer* (beggar), the facts and the picture had become more complex. The greater numbers of East and Central European Jews meant that their poor were more obvious and the proportion of street traders and itinerant beggars was probably greater than among the Sephardim.

* See Glossary

1820. 'Old clothes to sell'
Jewish old-clothes man in typical costume

Certainly, it was obvious to contemporary observers that poor-looking Jews were predominant in the street trades in London. Anglicised Jews added their voices to the chorus of English gentlemen who deprecated the nuisance of noisy Jewish street traders who 'embrace the most pitiful and mean employments to procure food, such as buying and selling old clothes, buckles, buttons, sealing wax, oranges and lemons or such like'.[6] Robert Southey complained about the 'Hebrew lads who infest you in the streets with oranges and red slippers or tempt schoolboys to dip into a bag for gingerbread nuts'. In the late eighteenth century and well into the nineteenth the most characteristic Jewish street trade was the buying and selling of old clothes. Although of low status, it was a necessary and thriving business at a time when the urban poor could not afford new clothes. In both the East and West End of London, the Jewish old clothes men bought from the rich, or from their servants, and sold to the poor. There were only about a thousand Jews in London at the time of the opening ceremony of the Bevis Marks Synagogue in 1701. By the end of the eighteenth century they numbered between 10,000 and 15,000.[7] The total Jewish population of England was certainly no fewer than 12,000 and could have been as many as 20,000, but it is generally agreed that three-quarters of the total were in London.

Outside London, small communities of Jews were to be found in many ports and coastal towns such as Chatham, Portsmouth, Plymouth, Liverpool, Yarmouth, Hull and King's Lynn as well as in many market towns further inland. These communities could not always support a Rabbi, let alone a synagogue, and consequently regarded the Rabbis of the established synagogues of London as their religious leaders. In particular, for the Ashkenazim, the Rabbi of the Great Synagogue was looked upon as 'Chief Rabbi' or as Rabbi Schiff of the Great (from 1765) styled himself, 'Rabbi of London and the Provinces'. For its rival, the Hambro', this was at first a bone of contention, and their Rabbi claimed the same grand title. Eventually, the Rabbi of the Great, the older synagogue prevailed and its Rabbi became the acknowledged spiritual head of the Ashkenazim. The Haham of the Sephardim remained as their Chief Rabbi.

In spite of the sporadic outbreaks of violent anti-Semitism – often a mixture of hostility to aliens and immigrants engendered by the wars against the French as much as hatred of Jews – England had become a country where Jews were generally tolerated. The nineteenth-century Jew, however, was not content to be merely unmolested and just tolerated: he wanted to be a citizen, with the full rights of an emancipated Englishman. It was a long struggle to gain those rights, and Jews had to wait longer than the Catholics or the Nonconformists for the removal of their disabilities. In the 1820s a Jew could not vote or be elected to Parliament, could not be called to the Bar nor be admitted to the only two universities in England, Oxford and Cambridge (the University of London had not yet been established). The City of London still barred him from becoming a freeman, which prevented him from trading in most of the Exchanges, and no Jew could hold a municipal office or an office of profit under the Crown.

The Repeal of the Acts preventing Catholics and Dissenters from entering Parliament in 1828 and 1829 left the Jews conspicuously alone in their disenfranchisement. It was clear, however, that the reforms were not going to be brought about 'on the coat-tails' of the Non-conformists: the Anglo-Jew would have to campaign actively on his own behalf to achieve full emancipation. The struggle gained ground steadily from the 1830s onwards. The restrictions on Jewish trading in the City of London were the first to go; in 1831 Jewish merchants and financiers were officially allowed to deal openly and expand their already growing concerns. The legal profession began to open its doors in 1833 when the first Jew was called to the Bar. University College, London, received its Royal Charter to grant degrees at about the same time (1835), and the University of London began its policy of admitting anyone who could afford it, regardless of creed or sex. This important educational opportunity, which broke the Oxbridge monopoly, made it possible for Jews to enter many professions other than those in commerce and finance. By 1845, Jews were able to hold any position or office in municipal authorities.

Most significant of all in the eyes of the Anglo-Jewish community was the election in 1847 of Lionel de Rothschild as a Member of Parliament for the City of London. It was the beginning, not the end, of the struggle to enter the House of Commons. He was barred from taking his seat because he was unable to take the Parliamentary oath 'on the true faith of a Christian'. During the next eleven years a number of Bills were passed by the Commons removing the necessity of taking this form of oath, but each Bill was thrown out by the House of Lords. Not until 1858, when a compromise was worked out, was Rothschild able to take his seat in the Commons.

By the late 1870s, there were about 60,000 Jews in England, more than half born in this country and therefore British. What were most of them like socially, culturally and economically? They had already acquired characteristics which distinguished them as British rather than European Jews. Only recently emancipated, they still suffered social and educational handicaps. Most of them were ill-educated, poor and lacking in the literacy and religious culture that characterised much of German and Austro-Hungarian Jewry. (The leading Rabbis in Anglo-Jewry had been born and educated in Europe.) The English that they spoke was nearer to Cockney or the local dialect than to the Queen's English. The most successful Anglo-Jews were exceptional individuals like Lionel de Rothschild, the City's leading banker as well as the first MP; Sir Moses Montefiore, the philanthropist and former Sheriff of the City of London, 'the most famous Jew of the century'; Sir David Salomon, former Lord Mayor of London and founder of the Westminster Bank, and others, members of leading Sephardi families like the Mocattas.

From the Orthodox view, British Jewry was lax and lacking in Jewish observance. Emancipation always tends to lead to assimilation and the relative freedom of Britain was already beginning to break up the closeness and the traditional ways of the Jewish family and its Jewish practices. On the other hand, there was a growth in the institutional strength of the synagogue in the late Victorian period. The United Synagogue was founded in 1870 and with it came the strengthening of the authority of the Chief Rabbinate. To a Jew from Central or Eastern Europe, the United Synagogue seemed a very English institution. Its synagogues seemed more like cathedrals and its Rabbis were beginning to look and sound like bishops. Until the 1880s, Jews in England were on the whole proud to be, or hoped to become, 'Englishmen of the Jewish persuasion'.

After 1880, Anglo-Jewry was profoundly changed by events in Russia and Poland. The notorious pogroms in Kiev and Odessa and the persecution in Poland led to a flood of refugees desperate to escape, hoping to sail to the 'Golden Land' – America – but willing to accept England as the next best destination. The effects of this massive influx of East European Jews on the small settled communities of London and the Provinces were far-reaching. Before 1870, the Anglo-Jewish population numbered about 50,000–55,000, mainly immigrants from Holland and Germany with an older settled community from Spain and Portugal. From 1881 to 1914, nearly 150,000 Jews entered Britain from Eastern Europe and Russia. The Anglo-Jews, who were becoming middle-class and respectable, resented the newcomers, those 'foreign Jews'. At first, when it was regarded as dealing with an emergency, the synagogues responded with money and food; the Board of Guardians dispensed relief to the immigrants but tried to discourage other Jews from coming. (The Board was sparing in its aid: a Jew had to have been in this country six months before he could even be considered for relief.) When it was realised that the problem was growing and not a passing phase, Anglo-Jews became hostile, and even eminent Rabbis tried to put up barriers or shunt the refugees on to other countries. A leading British Jew, N.S. Joseph, a respected member of the Board of Guardians and a distinguished figure in the United Synagogue, wrote in the *Jewish Chronicle* (June 1892): 'This class [the immigrants] constituted a grave danger to the community. Its members were always paupers and useless parasites in their own country. Many of them were never per-

secuted but came with the persecuted. If accepted as immigrants in England, they remain paupers and parasites and live or starve on the pittance that the Board of Guardians bestow on them . . .'.

Nevertheless, they kept coming, and most of them were here to stay. The Anglo-Jewish community grew fourfold in the 30 years after 1881. Thus middle-class Anglo-Jewry was vastly outnumbered in one generation by working-class, poor and traditionally Orthodox Jews of a very different linguistic and cultural background. Most of them spoke Yiddish, and came from the ghettos of Warsaw, Kiev and other large towns. The rest had been used to the *shtetl*, the small settlements, the village life of Eastern Europe and most had been overwhelmed by the cultural shock of arriving in a metropolis like London. The immigrants could not afford to join, nor did they feel comfortable in, the large synagogues of the United Synagogue. They set up *chevrot*, small club-like places where they met and worshipped all over the East End: the Vilna, the Wlodowa, the Dzikover, the Plotzner, Chevra Shass, the Kehal Chassidim, and scores of others in the back streets and alleys of Stepney and Mile End.

At first the Jewish establishment objected to this 'alarming' mushrooming of *chevrot*. In their view it would exacerbate the isolation of the immigrants and perpetuate their alien habits. The over-riding need was to Anglicise them to make them acceptable to England and to the Anglo-Jewish community. The *Jewish Chronicle* in January 1890 spoke unequivocally on behalf of the settled Jews: 'The Chevrot originate partly in the aversion felt by our foreign poor to the religious manners and customs of English Jews . . . The sooner the immigrants to our shore learn to reconcile themselves to their new conditions of living, the better for themselves. Whatever tends to perpetuate the isolation of this element in the community must be dangerous to its welfare'. The *Jewish Chronicle* first mooted the idea of a Federation of Chevrot, a suggestion which met with strong objections from some rabbis at first, but in fact was proposed and implemented by Sir Samuel Montagu, the moving spirit behind the creation of the Federation of Minor Synagogues in 1887.[8]

In the longer run, Anglicisation was largely effected through the schools. The Jews' Free School played an important role: originally a Talmud Torah, it was re-organised in 1817, and with considerable help from the Rothschilds it grew rapidly with the influx of new immigrants and by 1900 had 4,300 children within its classrooms. From being primarily religious it became increasingly secular. It was the largest but not the only school of its kind; there was the Westminster Jews' Free School and many similar schools in Manchester, Liverpool and Birmingham with about 8,000 pupils between them. After the Education Act of 1902 which made secondary education free and available to all up to 14 years, secondary schools and grammar schools began to take an increasing number of Jewish pupils with the help of scholarships and grants from the local authorities. Jewish boys even began to outnumber the non-Jews in some of the older grammar schools of the East End like Raines and Davenant (the Whitechapel Foundation), Cowper Street and others. Such schools had a profound influence on their Jewish pupils in providing a liberal or even 'classical' education in a Christian atmosphere. In such surroundings, Anglicisation was remarkably effective. Soon there were those whose unease at the process echoed the feeling of the Rabbi who used terms that were to become familiar as the twentieth century wore on: 'My spirit grieves that many have not joined and do not join any synagogue or Chevra and thus do not come throughout the year to worship . . .' (Dayan Spiers). But the Rabbis could not blame Anglicisation alone for the decline in religious observance and the loss of communal solidarity. England, and particularly London, presented opportunities and temptations in a more open society than any of the immigrants had ever experienced. Powerful economic pressures drew them into working on the Sabbath, which often made the difference between the survival of their new workshop or its collapse. As soon as they could, the immigrants became self-employed in tailoring, cabinet-making, hairdressing, selling in the street markets and in any opening that did not need much capital outlay. As some of them succeeded they moved out of the East End into a 'better class' of neighbourhood, usually to the northern suburbs (Highbury, Stoke Newington and Stamford Hill) or to the north-western districts of Maida Vale and St. John's Wood. Before long, economic factors began to blur the differences between the older Jewish communities and the new. By the 1930s, the Anglo-Jewish population was more dispersed and more divided by social class than by immigrant background.

The last significant influx came between 1933 and 1939: refugees fleeing from Nazi Germany and Austria. Although at least 75,000 came from Germany, they were more easily absorbed into the Anglo-Jewish community than the previous, much larger wave of immigrants from Eastern Europe. They were well-off and better educated; more than a thousand were scientists and academics, who were quickly absorbed into British universities and industrial research. They widened the scope of the professions penetrated by Jews, and helped to develop the newer industries in pharmaceutical products and light engineering. The refugees influenced and revitalised most of the synagogue movements in this country. The Reform Movement had been strong in Germany, and the ministers trained in that movement brought new ideas and set up new synagogues in Liberal and Progressive Judaism. On the right, the Orthodox movement that had kept apart from the United Synagogue was strengthened by the followers of the German Rabbis, especially Samson Raphael Hirsch. In fact, the German refugees came from the various strands of progressive and Orthodox Judaism and brought new vigour that contributed in a positive way to the existing institutions.

Jews in London

Throughout the centuries, both before the Expulsion and after the Resettlement, London has always been the centre of Anglo-Jewish life. Whether there were 10,000 Jews in Britain or nearly half a million (as in the mid-twentieth century) more than two-thirds made their homes in the capital. It is not difficult to explain the overwhelming attraction of London to Jews. It was, of course, the principal port of entry for successive waves of immigrants from Europe. Most of the immigrants entered England through the London docks and the majority settled nearby in the East End. London as the seat of the British government dominates the political and economic life of England. It was until recently the international centre of commerce, banking and finance, and still has one of the largest stock markets in the world.

Since the 1930s, the Jewish population has spread out, like London itself, into the new suburbs, especially those areas of Middlesex and Essex opened up by the Underground. The patterns of distribution depended to some extent on income and occupation: working-class Jews moved out of the East End to the northern and eastern suburbs (Haringey, Enfield and Redbridge). The middle- and lower-middle-class Jews tended to follow the Northern Line of the Underground and settled increasingly in Golders Green, Hendon, Edgware, Hampstead Garden Suburb, and Finchley. The vast areas of south London attracted very few Jews partly because commuting was more difficult from the southern districts to their places of work and business and these areas lacked local industry that could offer them a livelihood. Today the Borough that has the largest number of Jews is Barnet with around 48,000. Hackney in north London, which

Completing the writing of the Torah, Mill Hill Synagogue

for most of this century seemed a Jewish area, now has only 17,000. The Jewish East End has all but disappeared: in the Tower Hamlets, which include Whitechapel and the whole of Stepney, there are only 7,500 ageing Jewish residents, a mere 5 per cent of the total population in the Borough.

The Jews in Britain are not only urban people, they are predominantly metropolitan with a strong tendency to seek their homes in the suburbs where other Jews live. Increasingly, they move out of the inner city areas to the garden suburbs of London and other cities like Manchester, Leeds or Glasgow where they have settled. Of the total Jewish population of 300,000, some 200,000 or 66 per cent live in the capital. Small, perhaps, in comparison with the Jewish population of New York, but larger than that of any other city in Europe. It is a significant fact that the Jewish Londoner is in the minority even in those districts of London

where he is most conspicuous. Barnet, which includes Golders Green, Hendon and Edgware, has, as we have seen, by far the largest concentration of Jews in London. Although in the borough as a whole the proportion of Jews to the total inhabitants does not exceed 45 per cent, in certain areas such as Golders Green the proportion of Jews is as high as 70 per cent. Overall, however, London Jews are a minority.

Notes

1. A.M. Hyamson, *A History of the Jews in England* (London: Methuen, 1928), Ch.2, pp.15–16.
2. Ibid., Ch.7, p.55.
3. Ibid., Ch.2, p.16.
4. Ibid.
5. *The Diary of Samuel Pepys*, 14 October 1663.
6. Anon., *A Peep into the Synagogue*.
7. There are various estimates and no exact figures available.
8. See full description in Chapter 2, 'The Synagogue Movements'.

2

The Synagogue Movements

The Sephardim

Anglo-Jewry is no longer simply divided into two communities: the Sephardic Jews of Spanish and Portuguese origin and the Ashkenazim from Central and Eastern Europe. As in Israel, so in England, Sephardi has come to mean a Jew of Oriental origin, whether from India or Iraq, or the older settled communities of Spanish and Portuguese Jews. Indeed, in London and in Britain as a whole, Oriental Sephardis now outnumber Anglo-Jews of Spanish and Portuguese ancestry. No one knows exactly how many Oriental Jews there are in Britain. Estimates vary from 35,000 to 40,000 – about one-tenth of Anglo-Jewry. The Iraqis are the largest community, followed by those of Indian origin. There are at least 5,000 from Iran; 2,000–3,000 Moroccans and a similar number from Aden (called 'Adenis'), with smaller groups from Egypt and the Sudan. The old-established, more Anglicised Spanish and Portuguese Sephardim have only recently begun to recognise the existence of the Oriental Jews and to include them in Anglo-Jewish affairs.

The Spanish and Portuguese community and their synagogues have a reputation for elitism and exclusiveness which dates back to the days when relatively few wealthy families dominated their world. It used to be said that in order to join the Bevis Marks congregation, one had to be born into it, or married into it. This is no longer true but some sense of belonging to 'a better class of person' lingers on in the Anglo-Sephardic congregations.

Sephardic synagogues are strictly governed by their traditional book of constitutional law, the Ascamot. It was, indeed, the rigidity of the Ascamot, among other factors, that led to the breakaway from the Bevis Marks congregation and the formation of the Reform Movement in Britain.[1]

The first by-law of the Ascamot forbade the formation of any new synagogue within six miles of Bevis Marks; the setting-up of the West London Synagogue by some leading members of the Bevis Marks congregation led to their excommunication.

The Sephardi synagogue is run by a Board of Elders and a 'Mahamad' of five members who act as the executive of the congregation; the ordinary members are called the 'Yehidim' who pay a *finta* (annual assessment) regulated by the Ascamot.

Although Bevis Marks, the oldest synagogue in Britain, still maintains its special position as the parent synagogue of the Sephardic community, it probably attracts more tourists than worshippers these days. The most important synagogue of the Spanish and Portuguese Sephardim is in Maida Vale (W9) at the Lauderdale Road Synagogue. The Rabbi of both Bevis Marks and Lauderdale Road, Dr A. Levy, is now referred to as the Communal Rabbi of the Sephardic Congregation. Rabbi Levy, who was born in Gibraltar, is well aware of the diversity of backgrounds of his congregations; he has claimed to have 'the most colourful community in the country'.

Sephardi synagogues are to be found in Holland Park with its special links with the Turkish and Greek Jews, and as far apart as Wembley and Ilford.

The Jews of Middle Eastern origin have the Aden Jews' Congregation at Clapton Common (E5) and the Iranians worship at the Persian Hebrew Congregation in Stamford Hill. The Indian community have synagogues in Golders Green, Hendon and in Stamford Hill and their own *yeshiva** in Hendon run by Rabbi Abraham David from Rangoon.

* See Glossary

Bevis Marks, City of London

The Sephardim can claim to be both the oldest Jewish community in England and the newest. Their connections with Jewish communities beyond Europe have given Anglo-Jewry unique opportunities to gain insights into the great variety of cultural and religious traditions that make up world Jewry.

The United Synagogue

To most British Jews, the United Synagogue is the Establishment. Lord Jacobovits, the former Chief Rabbi, is the first holder of that office to be elevated to the peerage. He inherited and passed to his successor, Dr Jonathan Sacks, the grand title of Chief Rabbi of the United Hebrew Congregations of the British Commonwealth. The Chief Rabbi, the head of the

United Synagogue, is generally recognised as the official spokesman of Anglo-Jewry and its spiritual leader. Not everyone, however, is aware that the United Synagogue is an association of London synagogues whose congregations are Orthodox and Ashkenazi in origin. The 'U.S.' grew out of the original City of London Synagogues – the Great, the Hambro' and the New – and came into being officially in 1870 by Act of Parliament. One hundred years later, it had grown to be the largest group of synagogues in Britain with 70 member congregations and providing religious and pastoral services for about 100,000 people in the Greater London area. In 1970, when the 'U.S.' was celebrating its centenary, it was still possible to say that it was 'serving the needs of the Jewish community of London'.[2] In recent years, its authority has been challenged by other smaller synagogue groups on the extreme 'right' (the Chasidim) and by the movements on the 'left' (the Reform and Liberal synagogues).

The Chief Rabbi (1904). Hermann Adler in clerical robes

The role and position of the United Synagogue has changed dramatically since its early days in the last quarter of the nineteenth century when it was a strong influence promoting the Anglicisation of the large numbers of immigrant Jews, mainly from Russia, Poland and Eastern Europe. The settled Anglo-Jewish Community was ambivalent or even hostile towards the newcomers. To their credit, however, the 'U.S.' did offer help to their fellow-Jews through existing synagogues and welfare organisations. The leaders of the 'U.S.' from its inception were an élite, a close-knit group who dined together, who shared the same outlook and were accustomed to making decisions without much consultation of the wider community. This was the period of the 'cousinhood' (or as it was sometimes called, the Grand Dukes of Anglo-Jewry) who laid down the law for the benefit of their brethren. Despite their undemocratic ways, some of the Grand Dukes were enlightened enough to formulate practical measures to meet the challenges of the unprecedented problems of that period.

During the early years of the 'U.S.' it had to adjust to a great influx of Yiddish-speaking, poor, mainly Orthodox Jews with alien traditions, both religious and political. The newcomers included not only Chasidim (extremely Orthodox Jews devoted to their own Rabbis) but also anti-religious Socialist Jews who brought a new kind of Zionist nationalism into this country. The Orthodox Jews mostly rejected the United Synagogue with its English outlook. They had been used to the *shtiebl* in the *shtetl*, or in other words, the small homely, club-like congregation (the *chevra*) in the village community or in the ghetto in the city.

Although at first the 'U.S.' tried to prevent the spread of the East End *chevrot*, it was the far-sighted initiative of some of its leaders that helped to set up the Federation of Synagogues in 1887. For all its conservatism and middle-of-the-road Orthodoxy, the 'U.S.' has been a practical and positive force that has encouraged the growth of a great number of synagogues, meeting a variety of needs all over the Greater London area. It has provided the money and responded to the needs of many new congregations and has even been criticised for its emphasis on non-religious matters like buildings and plans for extensions. In its first century, it encompassed congregations like the Hampstead which was quite radical in its early days, as well as the more conventional Orthodox synagogues that were established in the north-western suburbs, from Willesden to Edgware, and in many other new suburbs. The United Synagogue today remains the religious parent organi-

sation for the largest section of Anglo-Jewry with a dominant role in its national institutions. The great U.S. synagogues of the West End may be in decline but the 'U.S.' is still very much alive in its many thriving congregations throughout Greater London and its outer suburbs.

The Federation of Synagogues

In the 1880s the correspondence columns of the *Jewish Chronicle* were full of letters about the 'alarming' growth of 'chevras' in the East End. It was in this period of strain between the new immigrant population and the settled Anglo-Jewish community that Samuel Montagu, a strictly Orthodox Jew, came forward with constructive proposals to bring some order into a chaotic situation. Montagu, although a leading member of the 'U.S.' establishment, understood the East End Jew and his hostility to the 'Grand Dukes', especially the Chief Rabbi, Dr Hermann Adler, who wanted to destroy the basis of the *chevra*. Samuel Montagu offered money and provided the services of an architect to bring together the various small *shuls* or 'Minor Synagogues', as he called them, into a voluntary association. As a result of his efforts, the Federation of Minor Synagogues was established in 1887. Small synagogues and *chevrot* were amalgamated, and those that did not meet minimum standards of size or hygiene were excluded. With Montagu's help, the new Federation built model synagogues in various parts of the East End.

Thus the Federation and the 'U.S.', both Orthodox and traditional in outlook and observance, came to exist separately but more or less in harmony. The issues that divided them have largely disappeared. It has been said that the Federation was 'the poor man's United Synagogue'[3] and there was some truth in the description in the early period and until the 1920s. The label, however, tends to obscure some of the deeper reasons for the existence of the Federation and its differences from the United Synagogue. The Federation was not only founded on the needs of the Ashkenazi immigrants of the 1880s and 1890s but also on their Orthodox practices and their Yiddish culture. They spoke Yiddish and expected their Rabbis to speak Yiddish when they were not praying or '*davaning*' in Hebrew. To some extent the typical Federation Synagogue and its core of members were more orthodox in matters of liturgy and cared more about strict observance of *kashrut* than their coreligionists in the United Synagogue. Certainly until the 1930s when Anglicisation had begun to change the second generation, there was greater resistance to change in the Federation.

When Zionism became an issue before and during the Great War, there were very strong feelings in the Federation which led to conflict and schism within their governing body and between their leaders and the ordinary rank-and-file members. It may seem curious now but there were many influential people in the Jewish community at that time (1916–17) who were strongly opposed to Zionism and disapproved of the efforts which culminated in the Balfour Declaration. In May 1917, the Joint Chairmen of the body representing the Board of Deputies and the Anglo-Jewish Association (on which the Federation was officially represented) published in *The Times* a manifesto against Zionism in which they attempted to dissociate the Jewish community from the movement. The second Lord Swaythling (the son of Samuel Montagu) came out publicly in support of the anti-Zionist manifesto. He was the President of the Federation and his action was bitterly resented by many in the East End, and the meetings of the Board of the Federation became stormy and torn by dissension. Lord Swaythling, unlike his father, the Founder of the Federation, was an Anglo-Jew out of touch with the majority of the East End Jews who were passionately in favour of Zionism. One feels that if the controversy had broken out in the United Synagogue, it might have been conducted with more decorum and more attention to parliamentary courtesies and procedure. The Federation member could not always express himself in appropriate English and did not care if he broke the rules of English public behaviour. The discontent with the leadership simmered on until it came to a head in 1925 when the second Lord Swaythling resigned. It was some time before a new and more generally acceptable president was found, but since 1928 (when Councillor M.H. Davis was elected President) the Federation has developed on more democratic lines and is more closely attuned to the feelings and more sensitive to the desires of its ordinary members.

The days when the typical member of the Federation was more devout than his counterpart in the United Synagogue have long since passed. Nowadays it is more a question of family association, of convenient accessibility or of preference for a smaller and more intimate congregation. The Synagogues of the Union of Orthodox Hebrew Congregations now cater for the ultra-Orthodox, and the *raison d'être* of the Federation has largely disappeared. There are, however, still 15 Constituent Synagogues and 20 affiliated congregations in Greater London, but many are in decline and some are not even open on the Sabbath. Nevertheless, those Federation Synagogues outside the East End, which serve communities in Ilford, Finchley, Golders Green and Edgware, are active and well-attended.

The Union of Orthodox Hebrew Congregations

The association of the most Orthodox synagogues in London is known collectively as the Adath and consists of about 50 congregations with about 6,000 members. Many of these synagogues are small and largely autonomous. Some, like the Stamford Hill Adath, are large and well-established, but many are really *shtieblach* – like the *chevrot* of an earlier period – meeting regularly in the back room of the Rabbi's home. Although their total membership is small compared with the congregations of the major synagogue movements, the Adath is a significant and growing force in the Jewish community. Even though they do not mix with the larger society of Anglo-Jewry, they seem, to many Jews in the mainstream of Orthodoxy, to be the standard-bearers, the embodiment of the traditional values of Judaism.

The Adath began in the 1880s as a reaction against the moderate United Synagogue type of Orthodoxy, personified in their eyes in the worldly views of the Chief Rabbis of that time, Hermann and Nathan Adler. The members were living in the Dalston and Stoke Newington districts of north London. In 1886 the Adath set up the North London Beth Hamidrash. In the early years of this century they established themselves in Stamford Hill, where a number of small congregations of similar views joined them under the leadership of Rabbi Dr Victor Schonfeld, an ardent follower of Samson Raphael Hirsch, the renowned Rabbi of Frankfurt. (Rabbi Hirsch had led a breakaway group against the trend towards Reform among German Jews.) In 1926 they formed the Union of Orthodox Hebrew Congregations which supports the Kedassia (kashrut authority), a Beth Din, and are linked to one burial society. The Union is, however, not centralised like the United Synagogue, as each constituent synagogue is self-governing and led by its own Rabbi.

In the past 25 years two distinct Orthodox types of synagogues have developed in north and north-west London: the Chasidim of north London, who follow their own form of service, and the Adath in north-west London (mainly Golders Green and Hendon), who still cling to the Frankfurt-Am-Main practices.

The Chasidim within the Adath movement tend to have their homes and their synagogues in and around Stamford Hill where they have been since the early days, a century ago when the first Beth Hamidrash was set up. It is obvious to any visitor to Stamford Hill that there are many Chasidim in the district. This has led some to call them the *schwartz* or 'black' Adath because of their black capote, their black hats or fur-trimmed *shtreimel*, black beards and side-locks. But the differences are deeper than their outward appearance. These Chasidic groups seem to create self-imposed ghettos and seek to maintain the kind of life which existed in the *shtetl* of Eastern Europe. They speak Yiddish as well as English, and religious duties and practice are at the centre of their lives. Unlike the 'white' Adath members, they are not only devout on the Sabbath; their Judaism is central and integral to their whole way of living.

In the closely regulated world of the Chasidim, the synagogue as a building is of little importance. The observance of the Sabbath, the daily services and the Festivals are the essential features, but their piety needs only simple surroundings and the basic requirements of the Jewish service: the prayer books, the Scrolls of the Law, some chairs and a table on which to place the Sacred Scrolls. The Holy Festivals and the Sabbath are not treated only with solemnity but with noise and rejoicing. A wedding is celebrated with seven evenings of feasting and dancing and fortissimo singing.

Whereas the Chasidic element in the Adath give the impression of rejecting the modern world, the non-Chasidic congregations in Golders Green, Hendon and Hampstead Garden Suburb attract successful professional people (barristers, university professors and scientists) and businessmen who want their synagogues to be uncompromising bastions of Orthodoxy, which demand full observance of Jewish ritual and law. In all Adath congregations there is the strictest division between men and women in the synagogue; women are not to be seen and are usually hidden behind screens or partitions. In some synagogues, there is a great mixture of Ashkenazim from various Eastern European backgrounds, and even some Chasidim who bring noise and bustle. The visitor may wonder at the apparent lack of respect and devotion in what seems an irreverent atmosphere. Yet the commitment is there, not only in the individual worshipper who 'davans' alone in the crowd, totally immersed in the prayers, but also in those periods during the long services when all the congregation join in the key passages of communal worship. Other Adath congregations,

like the Beth Hamidrash in Golders Green (known as 'Munk's'), are impressive for the dignity and piety of their worship. These are synagogues where the Rabbi's word is law and the service is conducted with great decorum.

In both types of Adath synagogue there is a dedication on the part of the members which other synagogue movements may well envy. The positive side of the Adath is this whole-hearted identification with the synagogue as *beth haknesset*, the meeting-place and *beth hamidrash* – the place for prayer and study of the Torah. It is not a separate entity – an institution – as the synagogue is often regarded in the United Synagogue and in the Reform Movement. On the negative side, one finds an intolerance of non-Orthodox Jews and a tendency to live in a closed world which is constantly on its guard against intrusions from the corrupt forces of our time.

The Reform Synagogues of Great Britain

The Reform movement is much older than the Liberal and Progressive synagogues and in ritual matters is more traditional and conservative. After all, the Founding Fathers of the first Reform Congregation were all members of the Orthodox Spanish and Portuguese Synagogue at Bevis Marks. They were highly respectable leading Sephardim – Montefiores, Henriqueses, Mocattas (nine members of the family) and Goldsmids. Not exactly a group of radicals. They were joined by six respected Ashkenazi members from the Great, the Hambro and the New – the other synagogues in the City.

Although the dissenters had tried to avoid extreme positions on doctrinal matters, they did feel dissatisfaction with the rigid traditions of Bevis Marks. They accepted the prohibition on travelling on the Sabbath, but were not prepared to walk every Saturday from their homes, which, increasingly, were in the West End and not in the City. This issue was at the heart of the matter although there was dissatisfaction with the *Siddur* – the Jewish book of common prayer. The services based on the *Siddur* were long and entirely in the sacred language, Hebrew. Some members had given up regular attendance and others had begun to feel disaffected as they found total opposition to change from the Orthodox Rabbinate.

The dissenting group of 18 leading members of the Bevis Marks congregation in 1840 stated their aims

Chasidim binding a new Scroll.

thus: to establish a congregation where 'a revised service may be performed at hours more suited to our habits and in a manner more calculated to inspire feelings of devotion, where religious instruction may be afforded by competent persons and where to effect these purposes, Jews generally may form a united congregation under the denomination of British Jews'.

These words were seen as a direct challenge to the Sephardic Synagogue and completely unacceptable. It soon became a doctrinal issue; the dissenters were denounced by the Sephardi Beth Din and their revised prayer book – albeit based largely on the Bevis Marks service – was totally rejected. At a meeting presided over by Sir Moses Montefiore, whose brother had joined the breakaway group, a solemn proclamation was issued declaring that 'certain persons calling themselves British Jews cannot be permitted to have any communion with us Israelites in any religious rite or sacred act'.

The formal act of excommunication announced by the Mahamad on 6 March 1842 invoked the first by-law of the Constitutional Laws of the Spanish and Portuguese Synagogue (the Ascama) which forbade the formation of any new synagogue within six miles of Bevis Marks. Thus, in spite of their limited aims, the dissenters were excommunicated, and this absolute rejection may well have led them into more radical departures from Orthodoxy than if they had been allowed merely to set up a branch of Bevis Marks nearer their homes.

The first synagogue of the Reform movement was established in Bruton Street in the West End; in 1870 it moved to its present home: the West London Reform Synagogue in Upper Berkeley Street. It has become one of the largest congregations in Britain.

Today, the most obvious differences between a Reform and an Orthodox synagogue are to be seen in the active participation of the women members in the service and in the use of English in the prayer book. In a Reform synagogue men and women sit together; women are called on to read parts of the service from the pulpit or from the *bimah*. There are even some women rabbis of Reform synagogues, an innovation which seems absurd or outrageous to the Orthodox. The Reform prayer books not only translate the Hebrew of the service – many Orthodox prayer books have done the same – but have introduced new 'readings' from European Jewish writers translated from other languages into English. Much of the service in many Reform synagogues is conducted in English but the *kaddish* (memorial prayer for the dead) and the *Shema* are recited in Hebrew. Another innovation was the introduction of the organ to accompany the reciting of prayers. Yet, in spite of the significant changes, the Reform synagogue, unlike the Liberal, tends towards the traditional in the form of the service.

The Reform movement generally regards itself as the modernised Anglicised version of the United Synagogue: as if it were the thinking Jew's updated orthodox synagogue. The Reform Movement began, after all, in the Orthodox Sephardic synagogue and was created by Orthodox dissenters. The other source of the Reform synagogue came later in the nineteenth century and in the 1930s when middle-class German refugees brought the ideas and practices of the German Reform Movement to England. Outside London, in Manchester and Bradford, Reform synagogues were founded to meet the needs of German-Jewish refugees who had set up textile factories and wholesale businesses in the North. Jewish families with a German Reform background could not easily fit into the Anglo-Jewish Orthodox synagogue; they wanted to become Anglicised but within a Reform congregation.

A number of factors have contributed to the growth of the Reform movement since the Second World War. Jews in London and elsewhere have become more suburban and less tied to the traditional Jewish areas of settlement associated with their immigrant background. They have moved out of the old trades of tailoring and small shopkeeping into the professions and commerce. And as they have moved out of the traditional ghettos and trades, the newer middle-class Jew marries 'out' increasingly. Assimilation has brought with it a rate of marriage with non-Jews estimated at about 30 per cent. Many Jews who have non-Jewish spouses try to bring them to a synagogue and often hope to be allowed to convert their partners to Judaism. Traditionally, the Orthodox Rabbinate does not encourage conversion and is insistent on complete adherence to Jewish practices by any applicant for conversion. The non-Orthodox Rabbinate, while not openly encouraging conversion, imposes fewer restrictions on their applicants, thus making conversion somewhat easier.

The assimilation factor and the greater mobility of Anglo-Jewry have produced a considerable growth in both the Reform and Liberal movements. Most of the 16 Reform synagogues in Greater London have been set up in the last 30 years. There is a great demand for Reform Rabbis and teachers for their religious schools. Jews' College, once the only Anglo-Jewish seminary, in its early days produced Ministers who served Reform congregations, but for the greater part of its history has concentrated on the Orthodox synagogues. In 1956 the

Reform Movement started its own Seminary which became the Leo Baeck College for the study of Judaism and the training of Rabbis, Ministers and Teachers. The College is now part of the Sternberg Centre, the headquarters of the Reform Movement of Great Britain.

The Liberal and Progressive Synagogues

The Union of Liberal and Progressive Synagogues represent a much more radical departure from traditional Jewish forms of worship than is to be found in the Reform Movement. Originally known as the Jewish Religious Union, it was founded by Claude Montefiore and the Hon. Lily Montagu (daughter of Samuel Montagu) in 1902. Although respected United Synagogues Rabbis like the Rev. Simeon Singer, Rev. A.A. Green and Rev. J.F. Stern associated themselves with it in its first year, they resigned as soon as they realised that the Founders were not just starting an independent movement with the vague aim of 'encouraging Judaism'. Montefiore conducted the services of the new Union without a hat or *talluth*, and with men and women sitting together. In 1909 it became 'The Religious Union for the Advancement of Liberal Judaism' and the Jewish press referred to it as a 'new sect' or even as a 'new religion'; The Chief Rabbi called it 'a menace to Judaism'.

Liberal Jews see their movement as a positive contribution to Jewish traditional values in a changing world. The Liberal Synagogue, in their own words, 'stresses ethics more than ritual, affirms the freedom and responsibility of the individual to act in accordance with his conscience and accords men and women equal status in the synagogue in marriage law'.

Although both the Reform and the Liberal synagogues tend to attract well-assimilated British Jews who cannot accept the traditional Orthodox forms of worship and their 'foreign' associations, there are significant points of difference between the two movements. The Liberal synagogue is more like some of its American counterparts in rejecting the old ways – Rabbi Mattuck, one of the founders of the Progressive Movement, once dismissed the whole corpus of dietary laws as 'an ancient Jewish prejudice'. The Reform Rabbi neither stresses nor rejects *kashrut*. The Reform service, generally, is similar to the Orthodox and all the 'key' prayers (the *Shema*, the *kaddish*) are in Hebrew. The number of passages and texts read in English varies from one Reform Synagogue to another. The Liberal service is mostly in English and is quite unlike the traditional form of worship.

The first Liberal Synagogue was opened in St. John's Wood in 1912 and the movement changed its name during the Second World War to the 'Union of Liberal and Progressive Synagogues'. It was, in fact, the fear of the Nazis that may have influenced the Chief Rabbi, Dr Hertz, in 1944, in certifying the Liberal Synagogue for the purpose of the Marriage Act.

In its early days, owing largely to the views of its Founding Father, C.G. Montefiore, the Liberal Movement was anti-Zionist. (The Reform Movement tended to be aloof and rather non-Zionist.) Montefiore's extreme opposition to Zionism, at least the Weizmann version which he disliked so strongly, was in the name of anti-nationalism. The positive thrust of his thinking was to show the world, Jew and Gentile alike, that Judaism was a universal religion and not a tribal creed. Of course, the Nazis, the Holocaust and the establishment of Israel, changed the position of all Jews, Liberal, Reform or whatever. The period after Montefiore's death in 1938 was one when there were no niceties for Jews; it was a question of survival.

Since 1945, the Liberal Movement has dropped its anti-Zionism and has concentrated on providing a Jewish form of Service that welcomes men and women on an equal footing, and they have been the first to appoint women Rabbis to some of their congregations. They are also hospitable to converts to Judaism. With the growth of inter-marriage among Jews who also tend to live in ethnically mixed areas, there has been a need for the non-Jewish spouse to be accepted into Jewish society through a synagogue. The Orthodox synagogues admit few converts.

The Reform and the Liberal synagogues admit many and are open to those who genuinely wish to convert. This factor alone has certainly contributed to the quite dramatic growth of both the Reform and the Liberal Movements in the past generation.

The headquarters of the Union of Liberal and Progressive Synagogues is at the West Central Synagogue in Whitfield Street, London, W1, and there are about a dozen Liberal Synagogues in London and its suburbs.

Notes

1. A detailed account is given in the section on the Reform Synagogues.
2. S.S. Levin (ed.), *A Century of Anglo-Jewish Life, 1870–1970* (London: United Synagogue, 1971).
3. C. Bermant, *Troubled Eden* (London: Vallentine, Mitchell, 1969).

3

Synagogues of the City of London and the East End

Bevis Marks: The Spanish and Portuguese Synagogue

'The Bevis Marks Synagogue is unique in Britain in its preservation and wealthy appointment'.[1] Bevis Marks is truly unique in its beauty which combines both English and Jewish decorative features. This splendid synagogue is admired not simply because it is old, but for its special place in the history of the Jews of London and of England.

The first Jewish synagogue of the period of the resettlement was no more than the upper floor of a house in Creechurch Lane, very near the present synagogue in Bevis Marks. It opened in 1656, and we get a glimpse of its lively congregation from Samuel Pepys who visited the small synagogue on 14 October 1663. The entry in the *Diary* shows his dismay at the strange behaviour of the Jewish 'men and boys in their vayles and the women behind a lattice out of sight . . . But, Lord! to see the disorder, laughing, sporting and no attention but confusion in all their Service, more like brutes than people knowing the true God . . .'. Pepys appears to have had no idea that he was witnessing a Festival Service for Simchat Torah when it is appropriate to sing loudly and dance and be riotously joyful.

By the end of the century, the Sephardic Congregation was too large for the little synagogue in Creechurch Lane and plans were made in 1695 for a new 'purpose-built' house of worship in Bevis Marks. The Wardens of the Congregation gave the contract for the construction of a new synagogue to a Quaker, Joseph Avis. The cost was to be £2,650 – quite a large sum at that time – about half of which was to be raised in contributions from the 'Yehidim', as the members of the Sephardi Congregation are called. The new synagogue

was completed and opened in September 1701, to the great joy of the congregation. It is said that Mr Avis returned to the Wardens 'such profit as he had made' on the day of the opening; he felt as a Quaker that he should not accept any financial gain for the 'building of a House of God'. Another story associated with this memorable occasion is that Princess (later Queen) Anne presented an oak beam from a Royal Naval vessel to be incorporated into the roof of the building.

The exterior of the synagogue has the simple proportions and appearance of many dissenters' chapels of that period. It is the interior that is distinctive, although much influenced by its impressive sister synagogue in Amsterdam, from which it gained one of the magnificent seven brass chandeliers. These great hanging candelabra, representing the seven days of the week, are still used on holy days to light the interior with candlelight. The splendid wooden Ark, resembling a reredos, is built in the classical baroque style typical of the time and has as its central feature the Ten Commandments in Hebrew. An unusual feature of the building is that on all four sides it has high rounded windows and the thickness of the walls can be seen by the width of the window recesses.

Much of the decorative ornamentation embodies a simple symbolism. Apart from the seven candelabra, there are six great brass candlesticks in front of the Ark (with the inscriptions of the donors 'P.M. & R. PEREIRA') and four more on the reading desk, making ten in all, to symbolise the Ten Commandments, while the twelve columns supporting the gallery are intended to represent the Twelve Tribes of Israel.

During its long history the congregation has had many famous and remarkable members among whom were David Nieto, Isaac d'Israeli, Moses Montefiore and Daniel Mendoza. David Nieto (1654–1728) was

Ner Tamid (eternal lamp) at Bevis Marks

Haham D. Nieto (1654–1728)

Haham (Chief Rabbi) of the Sephardi Congregation from 1702 until his death. Born in Venice, he studied medicine at the University of Padua and later lived in Leghorn where he was Dayan (Judge), Preacher of the Congregation and a physician. Evidently a polymath, he was highly regarded inside and beyond the Jewish community as a philosopher, poet, mathematician and astronomer. Nieto was the first to fix the time for the beginning of the Sabbath in England. The learned Haham was not universally admired during his time at Bevis Marks; he became the centre of controversy after he preached a sermon which seemed to many in the congregation as heretical as the pantheistic teaching of Spinoza. His position was eventually vindicated only by the pronouncement of the authoritative Rabbi Zvi Ashkenazi of Hamburg. The inscription on his tombstone is an eloquent eulogy:

> Sublime theologian, profound sage, distinguished physician, famous astronomer, sweet poet, elegant preacher, subtle logician, ingenious physician, fluent rhetorician, pleasant author, expert in languages, learned in history.

Isaac d'Israeli's association with the congregation was not a happy one. He was chosen to be a Warden of the Congregation in 1813, an honour he refused to accept. According to the strict laws (the Ascamot) of the Sephardis, anyone who rejected the office was subject to a fine of £40. Rather than pay the fine, d'Israeli left the congregation; a few years later he decided to leave the Jewish community altogether and had his children baptised as Christians. As Jews were barred from becoming Members of Parliament until 1858, this quarrel and its consequences certainly made it easier for his son, Benjamin, to enter Parliament, and later become the first son of a Jew to be Prime Minister of England.

The most famous Jew of his time was a distinguished member of the Sephardi Congregation from the end of the eighteenth century to the end of his long life in 1885. Sir Moses Montefiore was so active in so many aspects of Jewish life in this country and in other countries that his life has been the subject of many books and numerous studies. Perhaps the best thing about this legendary figure was his use of his energy and time to give practical help to, and indeed rescue, persecuted Jews anywhere in the world. In the nineteenth century no-one, not even the wealthiest passenger, could avoid discomfort on land or especially at sea, but nothing could deter Moses Montefiore from setting off to Egypt, to Turkey, to Morocco or Russia.

Sir Moses Montefiore

He always believed in going to the top, to the heads of government or even to the Pope, to help Jews in trouble. In fact, one of his less successful missions was in connection with a Jewish child, in the Mortara affair, who was baptised without the knowledge of its parents and then abducted by the Papal Police to be brought up as a Christian. Sir Moses went to Rome but was refused an audience with Pope Pius IX, although a Cardinal did receive him and assured him that such a thing would not happen again. Sir Moses was a devoted member of the Bevis Marks Congregation and as an Orthodox Jew, always walked from his home in Park Lane to the old *snoga* in the City for the Sabbath Service. He was a great man but not always a tolerant one, and his role in the excommunication of those members of the congregation, including his own brother, who broke away and set up the first Reform Synagogue, has been described in another section (see page 36).

Daniel Mendoza (1763–1836) was another celebrated Jew connected with Bevis Marks who distinguished himself with his bare fists. He was the

Daniel Mendoza, from an engraving by Gillray

champion of England and, according to the historians of the sport, raised it from being a matter of brute force and survival to something more like 'the art of boxing'. It has been said that 'no pugilist whatever . . . has ever so completely elucidated or promulgated the principles of boxing as Daniel Mendoza'. The father of scientific fisticuffs continued practising 'the noble art' well into middle age. He was still boxing at the age of 57.

Today the synagogue is used for worship, although it is no longer the living centre of the Sephardic Community in London. The largest and most active of the Spanish and Portuguese Synagogues is to be found in Maida Vale at the Sephardi Synagogue in Lauderdale Road. Nevertheless, Bevis Marks is no mere monument, and its special place in the history of Jewish worship still draws Jews from many different kinds of synagogues for important occasions and Festival Services.

The first time I attended a service in the old *snoga* was in 1985, during the Board of Deputies Festival of British Jewry when I sat inside the beautiful building and listened to the traditional melodies sung by the Sephardi Choir. The high-backed wooden pews were not very comfortable but one scarcely noticed the hard seats for the delight of experiencing a service in candlelight surrounded by gleaming symbols of Judaism in a synagogue of such mellow beauty. Jews have few houses of worship that can compare with the great cathedrals of England.

It is therefore with special pleasure that one attends a service in our venerable Anglo-Jewish Synagogue in Bevis Marks. Curiously, it is both English and Jewish and the strange mixture works a kind of magic on the sympathetic eye. The building itself, designed by a seventeenth-century Quaker, is restrained, dignified and well-proportioned. The decoration and the ornaments are traditionally Jewish and full of meaningful symbols of our ancient religion. It is fitting that this fine synagogue has survived and should be a matter of pride to all Londoners – Jew and non-Jew alike.

The Great Synagogue

'One of the world's most famous Jewish congregations – the Great Synagogue in London.'[2] The special place that the Great holds in Anglo-Jewish history cannot be accounted for simply in terms of the two and a half centuries of its life, nor that it was the first synagogue for the Ashkenazim in England after the Resettlement. Its importance lies rather in its having become the centre of a community that extended throughout the

The Great Synagogue, 1809

The Great Synagogue at Duke's Place, 1722: The Jewish manner of holding up the Law in the sight of the people

metropolis and beyond; moreover it was the nucleus around which the United Synagogue Movement was formed. The Rabbi of the Great became recognised and accepted as the Chief Rabbi of all British Jewry and the spiritual leader of Jews in Britain and the British Empire. Its special position as the Mother Synagogue came about gradually from its early days until the height of its power and influence towards the end of the nineteenth century.

Shortly after the opening of the Spanish and Portuguese synagogue in Creechurch Lane, a house of worship for the German Jews in London was founded in 1690. The congregation met in a house in Duke's Place, and there the Great remained, in spite of changes and reconstruction, until the end came in the Second World War. Among the founding fathers, the most prominent was Benjamin Levy, a wealthy merchant whose son Elias later became Warden of the Great. Elias married Judith Hart, the daughter of Moses Hart, the man whom many regard as the real founder of the

Great Synagogue. The first Rabbi of the congregation was Judah Leib Ben Cohen, who did not keep his position for long. He came into conflict with the learned Reb Aberle (also known as Reb Hamburger), an intolerant Elder of the community and one of its founders. Rabbi Cohen felt constantly under criticism from Reb Aberle and the rest of the congregation and at the earliest opportunity escaped his 'persecutors' by taking a position as Rabbi in Rotterdam. The early years of the Great were often marked with disputes and schisms. The most serious came in 1707 when a secession led to the formation of the second Ashkenazi synagogue in London, the Hambro'.

In spite of dissension, the congregation grew and the Great became the senior synagogue of the Ashkenazi community in London. To a remarkable extent, it owed its development throughout its first century to one family: the Harts (their original name was Hertz, although they were also known as the Hartwigs of Hamburg). Aaron, brother of Moses Hart, had the key role of Rabbi of the Great throughout the half century from 1704 to 1757. Having made his fortune as a broker and government agent in stocks, Moses was determined to establish himself as the undisputed leader of the Jewish community in the City. He became the synagogue's chief benefactor by consolidating the lease of the existing building and by ordering the construction of a properly designed house of worship, on the site at the south-east corner of Duke's Place. He bore the entire cost of the construction (£2,000). On the eve of the New Year (5483), 18 September 1722, the Great was dedicated. Although the building was reconstructed and enlarged twice after that time, the historic Great Synagogue of London was created by Moses Hart. A tablet in the forecourt acknowledges his unique contribution:

ON THIS SPOT OF GROUND MOSES HART LATE OF ISLEWORTH IN THE COUNTY OF MIDDLESEX DID IN HIS LIFETIME AND AT HIS SOLE EXPENCE Erect a synagogue . . .*

It is no wonder that the Great was known for many years as 'Moses Hart's Shul'.

Unfortunately, little is known about the design or appearance of the synagogue of 1722 (except what is shown in the engraving of its interior on page 43). We know only that it was smaller but similar in style to the nearby Bevis Marks.

Jews are rarely satisfied with one synagogue, no matter how small the community it serves. In spite of the bitter experience with the setting up of the Hambro', the authorities of the Great insisted on preserving their position. The German Jewish community continued to grow, and demands for change were not dealt with tolerantly or with understanding. Once again dissension led to a split, and another Ashkenazi synagogue was established in 1761 in Bricklayer's Hall in Leadenhall Street. True to form, the Rabbinate of the Great denounced the new congregation as 'a profanation of the Divine Name' and the leaders of the secession were expelled from the community. Nevertheless, a congregation was set up and became the New Synagogue. Thus London had a third synagogue for the Ashkenazi community.

After the experience with the New Synagogue, the leaders of the Great finally recognised that they could not expect to maintain their position as the senior congregation unless they could accommodate the rapidly growing Jewish population. In 1762, it was decided that Moses Hart's *shul* had to be enlarged and an extension of the site was acquired. In 1766, largely at

* The inscription also pays tribute to his daughter Judith Hart.

the expense of fifteen donors, the Great was rebuilt. We have no clear picture of these changes apart from two brief contemporary descriptions.

The Rev. Entick wrote: 'On the west side is the Synagogue of the Dutch Jews . . . This synagogue is just now enlarged with an addition of building in brick that makes it as large again as it was before; and has approached so near to the Church of St. James, Duke's Place that the congregations may be heard from each other'.[3] And just one telling sentence by Charles Wesley, the brother of the founder of Methodism, who visited the synagogue a year or so after it opened: 'The place itself is so solemn that it might strike an awe upon those who have any thought of God'.

Within less than a generation, the Great had to face yet another reconstruction. Persecution and ghetto life in Central and Eastern Europe caused a continuous flow of Continental Jews into London, where conditions for the practice of their religion seemed good and safe. The Great simply could not meet the demand for seats and membership. Two more adjoining plots of land were acquired but this time the necessary finance was more difficult to raise. In the 1770s the congregation had had to borrow by means of a mortgage on their building and their financial position was not strong.

Mrs Judith Levy: 'the Queen of Richmond Green'

At this crucial time another member of the Hart family appeared with the means to enable a radical re-building of the Great. The benefactor was a very unusual lady, Mrs Judith Levy, second daughter of Moses Hart. She was not an orthodox Jewess and indeed her circle of friends were mainly Gentiles, but her connection with the synagogue through her family was deep and long-standing. Besides her father, her father-in-law, Benjamin Levy, had been a principal founder of the first congregation, and her husband Elias had been very active in the running of the synagogue. Elias died young, but his widow survived him for 53 years. After his death she bought a house on Richmond Green (No. 4 in the elegant terrace still known as Maids-of-Honour Row) where she remained until the end of her long life. She was known as 'The Queen of Richmond Green' owing to her lavish style of entertaining and her generosity. It is said that she gave at least a thousand pounds a year to charity, even though she became a recluse in old age. Her reputation as an eccentric *grande dame* seems to have been based on her kindness to her servants; she allowed them coffee and tea which were regarded as luxuries in the eighteenth century. This remarkable lady gave £4,000 to the building fund of the Great – twice as much as her father had given for the first synagogue. This made it possible for the congregation to re-design and totally rebuild the Great.[4]

James Spiller, a fashionable architect, was engaged to design the new building. It was completed in 1790 and accommodated more than 500 men and 250 women; the building itself cost £12,402.10s.5d, and a further £2,000 was spent on furnishings. The new Ark, reading-desk and seating alone amounted to £4,000, that is, as much as the whole of 'Moses Hart's shul'.[5]

The Great Synagogue became one of the sights of London. In Remnant's *London* of 1793, attention was drawn to 'The Jews' Synagogue in Duke's Place which has been lately rebuilt in a beautiful style of the simplest Grecian architecture by Mr Spiller, architect'. A more detailed description appeared in *Views of London* (Partington, 1834): 'The building is of brick with a roof supported by massive stone pillars ... The utmost magnificence is exhibited. From the ceiling are suspended seven modern highly-finished brass branches of peculiarly excellent workmanship ...'. The Great Synagogue had become a large and eminently suitable edifice for the central 'cathedral' of Anglo-Jewry. During the nineteenth century it needed restoration and renovation but essentially the structure and design of 1790 lasted and served it well. It had become much more than a large, stately synagogue. No other syna-gogue had such a powerful appeal and such a hold on the feelings of the majority of Anglo-Jewry.

In 1870, when the United Synagogue was formed by the Great and four other major synagogues (the Hambro', the New, the Central and the Bayswater), the status of the Great was profoundly altered. In a sense, however, its real significance as the parent synagogue was officially recognised. By the creation of the United Synagogue and the recognition of the Rabbi of the Great as Chief Rabbi, it was seen by all Anglo-Jewry as the Mother Synagogue with daughter congregations in other parts of London. The Great could no longer be considered as a place of worship restricted to the City and the neighbouring districts of the East End.

This beautiful and historic synagogue was a victim of the Second World War. On 11 May 1941, the Great Synagogue was totally destroyed by fire during a bombing raid on the City of London.

The Hambro' Synagogue

Of the three historic City of London Synagogues set up by the Ashkenazi community, least is known of the Hambro's original building. No engravings exist and all we have are some photographs of the interior. Delissa Joseph, the architect of the buildings that were later erected on the site, had the photographs taken before the old Hambro' was demolished in 1892 (see illustration on page 46). It appears to have been similar in design to the Spanish and Portuguese Synagogue, perhaps owing to the congregation's antipathy to the Great and some tendency to favour the Bevis Mark's design. The Hambro's interior showed the traditional orthodox plan with central *bimah* and ladies' gallery on three sides supported on classical columns. The whole interior was richly furnished – the Ark being made of carved natural hardwood. There was seating for 218 men and 55 women. Some of the ritual objects can be seen on display in the London Jewish Museum at Woburn House.

The Hambro' came into being in the early years of the eighteenth century as a result of a split in the Great Synagogue. The leader of the secessionists was a prosperous gem-dealer called Mordecai (or Marcus) Moses, who as a young man had left his home in Hamburg to seek his fortune in London. Together with his friends and business associates, he wished to set up a Beth Hamidrash, a house of study with a small synagogue attached, on the lines of a well-known establishment in Hamburg. The move was bitterly opposed by Moses Hart and the leaders of the Great,

The Hambro', Fenchurch Street (1725–1893)

who enlisted the support of the head of the Spanish and Portuguese congregation to prevent the establishment of another Ashkenazi synagogue in the City. The leaders of the Great and the Sephardim even appealed for support to the Court of Aldermen of the City of London. The appeal was successful: the Court declared that 'they will not permit nor suffer the said place (a house in St. Mary Axe) to be converted into a Synagogue for the exercise of the Jewish religion . . .'.

The secession was suppressed but not the determination of Marcus Moses. The dispute had been aggravated by the refusal of Moses to accept a divorce arranged by Rabbi Aaron Hart (the Rabbi of the Great). This was not seen as a trivial objection but a heinous offence; it led to Marcus Moses being banned from the Congregation – in effect to his excommunication and boycott by the majority of the community. He appealed and gained the support of eminent Rabbis in Hamburg

and Amsterdam, who considered he had been treated unjustly. In open defiance of the rulings, Marcus Moses opened a synagogue in his own house in Magpye Alley, only a few hundred yards from Duke's place. He installed his family tutor, Johanan Hölleschau, as Rabbi, and furnished his home with the Scrolls of the Law and all the necessary ritual objects. In March 1707 the arrangements were completed and the total break with the parent synagogue was sealed by Moses' acquisition of a site in Hoxton as a cemetery for the new congregation. (The lease of the piece of ground was for 150 years at an annual rent of 10 shillings.)

The synagogue that started in Marcus Moses' house remained there for 22 years. In 1721, Mr Moses returned from his travels in the East with a large fortune and used it to begin the building of a proper synagogue in the garden of his house. The synagogue was completed in 1726 in Church Row (also called Magpye Alley) in Fenchurch Street, where it remained until the end of the nineteenth century. It was called the

Hambro' in honour of its founder, and his Hamburg origin.

The new Hambro' was not built in the City but in Whitechapel in the heart of the Jewish East End. The memorial stone was removed from the old Hambro' when it was demolished in 1892 and placed in the entrance of the new synagogue in Union Street, off Commercial Road. The building was designed by Lewis Solomon and opened in 1899; it was less distinguished than its predecessor. By all accounts, the interior was not well furnished and the whole building gave an impression that the Hambro' had come down in the world. The new building was, however, larger, seating 400 people. Its only remarkable feature was its Ark, which was so elevated that it needed an exceptional flight of steps for the worshippers to reach it.

The Hambro's second home in the East End had a shorter life than its first: ironically, it lost its independent identity when it was decided to reunite it with the Great, its parent synagogue, in 1936.

Sandy's Row Synagogue

In the middle of the nineteenth century when there were fewer than 20,000 Jews in the whole of London, a small group of Jewish immigrants from Holland established a working-men's *chevra*, a kind of religious Friendly Society in Spitalfields. The original Society, which later became the Sandy's Row Synagogue, was founded as 'Hevrath Menachem Avelim Hesed Ve'emeth' – a Society of Kindness and Truth. The major purpose of the *chevra* was to provide a traditional Jewish burial for even the poorest member. The 50 Dutch Jewish working men who formed the Society laid down that its purpose was to provide:

1 a *shivah* benefit of ten shillings during the week of mourning;
2 a *minyan* during shivah (i.e. ten men for Divine Service at the mourner's house);
3 payment to a rabbi to speak at morning and evening *shivah* services.

The Society used small rooms in the Spitalfields district and later the Zetland Hall in Mansell Street for High Holyday and other Festival Services. In 1867, 13 years after their foundation in 1851, they established the congregation in the French Chapel in Artillery Lane, Bishopsgate. By 1870 they had grown into a congregation of some 500 members (known locally as the 'Parliament Square Congregation') but they ran into opposition from the United Synagogue 'Establishment'. Their lease expired and £700 was needed to extend it, to repair the building and to create a new entrance in Sandy's Row. The congregation managed to raise £200 but then appealed to the wider Jewish community for help with the rest of the fund, which caused great opposition from leading Jews in the United Synagogue. They argued that there was no real need for a new synagogue in Spitalfields so near to the well-established City synagogues which had vacant seats that could be offered at reduced rates. The Sandy's Row members were incensed at the proposal and refused to become 'second-class members' of the City synagogues. In any case, they were convinced that their synagogue satisfied a real need in enabling Jews who were less affluent to run their own affairs and their own *shul*. The Sandy's Row Congregation overcame the opposition and managed to gather subscriptions totalling £350, which was just sufficient to preserve their building.

The impressive ceremony of consecration was conducted by the Haham (the religious leader of the Sephardi Congregation). The Chief Rabbi, Dr Nathan Marcus Adler, refused to attend owing to the controversy and the vexed question of giving encouragement to the growth of small independent synagogues.

Two very different accounts of Sandy's Row in the 1880s give a sense of this small East End Synagogue in the latter part of the nineteenth century. First, a Jewish view, on 1 June 1888, the *Jewish Chronicle* described the Sandy's Row Synagogue as 'a model Chevra . . . with the providence of the Dutch this "minor synagogue" not only pays its way but it makes an annual grant of five guineas to the Hospital Sunday Fund and two guineas to the Anglo-Jewish Association'. The second account is by a Gentile observer, Beatrice Potter (Mrs Sydney Webb):

> The heat and ardour convince you that the skylight is not used for ventilation. From behind the trellis of the ladies' gallery you see at the far end of the room the richly curtained Ark of the Covenant, wherein are laid, attired in gorgeous vestments, the Sacred Scrolls of the Law.
>
> Slightly elevated on a platform in the midst of the congregation stands the Reader or Minister, surrounded by the seven men who are called up for the Reading of the Law. Scarves of white cashmere or silk softly bordered and fringed are thrown across the shoulders of the men and relieve the dusty hue and disguise the Western cut of the clothes they wear. A low, monotonous but musical-toned recital of Hebrew prayers . . . rises from the congregation

Sandy's Row, Spitalfields, E1

while the Reader intones with a somewhat louder voice the recognised portion of the Pentateuch. Add to this the rhythmical cadence of numerous voices, the swaying to and fro of the bodies of the worshippers . . . and you may imagine yourself in a far-off Eastern land. But you are roused from your dream. Your eye wanders from the men to the small body of women who watch behind the trellis. Here, certainly, you have the Western world, in the bright-coloured ostrich feathers, large bustles and tight-fitting coats of cotton velvet or brocaded satinette. At last you step out, stifled by the heat and dazed by the strange contrast of old-world memories of a majestic religion and the squalid vulgarity of an East End slum.[6]

By the end of the nineteenth century, Sandy's Row was firmly established; the synagogue was not only the spiritual home for Jews of Dutch origin in that part of East London, but its Netherlands Club was a social centre where a variety of cultural activities were held. It became a constituent of the Federation of Synagogues in 1887, but from 1899 it was associated with the United Synagogue for burial purposes. After the Second World War, in 1949, it regained its autonomy and remains today an Independent Congregation.

The Machzikei Hadath and The Spitalfields Great Synagogue – from Brick Lane to Golders Green

In September 1983 (just before the New Year 5744) a new synagogue was consecrated in Highfield Road in the suburban district of Golders Green in North-West London. This modern custom-built brick building opened a new chapter in the story of the Orthodox congregation which began nearly a century ago as the Machzikei Hadath (roughly translated: 'Upholders of the Faith').

In the 1890s a group of Ashkenazi Jews from Germany had formed the Beth Hamidrash in North London and joined forces with another strictly orthodox group known as the Chevra Shomrei Shabbat which was founded in 1890 to preserve the Holy Sabbath and above all to improve the *kashrut* standards in the Jewish districts of London. They were particularly concerned with the supplies of kosher meat and what they regarded as the flagrant disregard of the strict laws laid down by the Beth Din (the Jewish

religious court). The 1890s in Britain were a difficult time of contradictory trends: on the one hand it was a period of decline in religious observance among the more settled Anglo-Jewish population, but on the other, it was a time of rapid expansion with immigrants from Eastern Europe pouring into London and other cities, bringing significant numbers of Orthodox Jews. Many of these Jews found the ways of Anglo-Jewry too liberal and easy-going. It was against this background and in repudiation of the authority of the Chief Rabbi that a rival *kehilla* (community) was set up as the Machzikei Hadath in 1891. They acquired a fine Georgian building in Spitalfields on the corner of Brick Lane and Fournier Street which became known as the Spitalfields Great Synagogue, a landmark in the East End for the next half-century and widely regarded as the fount of Orthodox Jewish practice. It was undoubtedly one of the most important Orthodox Synagogues in England.

The Synagogue in Brick Lane occupied a former church known as the 'Neuve Eglise' erected in 1743 by French-speaking Huguenot refugees. In 1819, it was sold by the Huguenots and became a Wesleyan Chapel. Another religious conversion occurred in 1898 when it became the Spitalfields Great Synagogue and was leased to the Machzikei Hadath Community. The Georgian exterior was preserved but the interior was reconstructed as a synagogue by Maple and Co. at a cost of £4,500. The organ which was part of the Wesleyan Chapel was transferred to the Methodist Chapel in Hackney Road.

The Spitalfields Great consciously modelled itself on the East European synagogue as a *beth haknesset; that is* is, a meeting-place for Jews to pray and study – an 'ever-open *shul*'. In fact, the Machzikei Hadath as a synagogue was open all day and served as a centre of learning, a place of prayer and a 'source of spiritual leadership'. Rabbi Ridvuz, a renowned East European scholar, visited the Machzikei Hadath in its early years and wrote: 'I have prayed for close to two weeks in the synagogue of this holy community and I imagined that I was among the holy communities of Eishishock or Volozhin and not in the capital city of London'. One of its most famous rabbis was Rav Kook, a great Jewish scholar, who did not find England a congenial place – he called it 'a spiritual wasteland'. He stayed only three years as Rabbi of the Spitalfields Great, from 1916 to 1919, when he went back to Palestine and became Chief Rabbi in 1921. Other eminent Rabbis of the Machzikei Hadath have included Rabbi Aba Werner, Rabbi Yechezkel Abramsky, who was the Rav from 1932

The Spitalfields Great Synagogue, Brick Lane, E1

until he became a *dayan* (judge) of the Beth Din of London in 1935, and more recently, Rabbi Simcha Lopian.

The Machzikei Hadath continued to flourish at the Spitalfields Great Synagogue throughout the inter-war period but from the outbreak of the Second World War, it began to decline with the breaking-up of the Jewish East End. As the Jewish inhabitants moved away from the East End to the suburbs so the Machzikei Hadath had to consider another more appropriate home. For many years this proved impossible, in spite of the fact that the congregation had acquired a site in Golders Green after the war, in 1948. Undaunted by their lack of a synagogue building, they continued their services for 26 years at the home of the late Rabbi

Lopian in Golders Green. Eventually the foundation stone of the new synagogue was laid in January 1982 in Highfield Road, Golders Green. The Chief Rabbi, Dr Immanuel Jakobovits, in a letter which was read out on the occasion, recalled his memories in these words: 'The rebirth of the Machzikei Hadath Synagogue brings back precious personal memories to me. Not only did I frequently worship at the Machzikei Hadath in Brick Lane in the 1940s, but I was, on several occasions, privileged to deliver a sermon to what was then indeed a "Torah fortress in Anglo-Jewry"'.

Yet another conversion has occurred in recent years after the Machzikei Hadath closed the Spitalfields Great Synagogue in the 1950s: it is now a mosque and known as the London Jamme Masjid. Once again the exterior has not been altered but the fine gallery in the main hall has unfortunately been demolished.

The new Machzikei Hadath, Golders Green

The present home of the Machzikei Hadath is a modern building designed by Sir Charles Nicholson. A special feature of the construction is the roof above the Ark which can be opened to allow wedding ceremonies to take place 'under the sky' – an ancient Jewish tradition – without the congregation moving out of the synagogue. The new synagogue has twelve stained-glass windows, and all the pews were made in a kibbutz in Israel.

Although the 'Torah fortress' no longer occupies a unique position for the Orthodox Anglo-Jew, it is remarkable that it has not only survived but is thriving in its new home in Golders Green.

The Fieldgate Street Synagogue, E1

Nowhere is the great change in the East End of London more evident than in Fieldgate Street in the heart of the Jewish East End. This small but well-established synagogue is dwarfed by a large new domed mosque and minaret which dominate the street. The passers-by are mainly white-capped Asian Muslims, as this is now their district. Few Jews still remain as local residents. Those who call at the synagogue, apart from the members of the congregation, are likely to be American visitors seeking information about their families and their 'roots'.

The synagogue was set up in 1899, but the original building was damaged by bombs in the early part of the Second World War. The present building was recon-structed in 1950 as a close replica of the original. The congregation is affiliated to the Federation of Synagogues and seems to be alive and well, although it had difficulties in surviving in the period after the war. It has about a thousand members, scattered all over London and a few who have transferred from other East End synagogues when they had to close down. Member-ship is maintained by those who now live far away in the new suburbs, mainly for sentimental reasons or to secure burial rights.

The vitality of the congregation owed a great deal to the lively personality of the late Reverend L. Gayer who

*Fieldgate Street Synagogue,
Stepney, E1 (exterior)*

Fieldgate Street Synagogue (interior)

first came to the synagogue as the Minister in 1933. He kept the synagogue going by acting as Minister and President, Secretary and Treasurer. This small active synagogue offers daily services both in the morning and in the evening, and the Rev. Gayer usually gave a short talk on the *sedra** of the week during the Friday Evening Service. On Sabbath mornings there is a good attendance and invariably a *kiddush** with the wine and *challah* (bread) donated by one of the members. A special feature of the Sabbath Morning Service is the call of the muezzin from the mosque next door. In fact, the call rings through the synagogue every day at fixed times but only on the Sabbath does it coincide with the Morning Service.

The East London Synagogue, Stepney Green

It is quite a step from Aldgate to Stepney Green, which in recent years has regained some of its greenness. The area has now an odd mixture of suburban streets and semi-rural open spaces made possible by massive slum clearance after the devastation wrought by bombing in the Second World War.

The East London Synagogue in Rectory Square was built in 1876 by the architects, Davis and Emanuel. At first it was the only synagogue of significance east of the Great Synagogue in the City, and was an important religious and social centre. Through its first Minister, Joseph F. Stern, it played an influential role in the 'Anglicisation' of the immigrant Jews of the East End in the last decade of the nineteenth century and the early years of the twentieth.

Joseph Stern has been called an 'anomaly'[7] and there is certainly something curious about a man who devoted 40 years of his life to presiding over an East End Synagogue but always lived in Hampstead. He was a consciously Anglicised Minister, the first to wear a clerical collar. A renowned social worker among the poor Jews of the area, he was known as 'the Jewish Bishop of Stepney'. Neither a rabbinic nor a Talmudic scholar, he saw his role as a preacher and a pastor to his flock. A Victorian in many respects, Stern was an outspoken man who used the pulpit to exhort and morally uplift his congregation.

He was born in Bedford in 1865 and educated at the Stepney Jewish Schools and then at the school in Finsbury Square run by Nathan Adler (who later became the Chief Rabbi). His father, Frederick Stern, officiated as Reader of the small Chevra which grew

Reverend Joseph F. Stern

into the East London Synagogue. Stern was appointed to the synagogue in 1887 as Preacher, Second Reader and Secretary. His election was strongly opposed and he was chosen by only a small majority. From the first he made his strong personality felt and he brought in radical changes.

He was the first Minister to introduce special services for children which, after early opposition (it was thought by some traditionalists to detract from parental responsibility), became a model for synagogues generally. He disapproved of the kind of teaching at the nearby Talmud Torah in Redman's Road, which he regarded as a typically Eastern European *cheder** and a hotbed of political and cultural Zionism. Stern frowned upon the use of Yiddish which he regarded as a barrier to Anglicisation. He was by no means alone in this view, which was often heard from senior lay readers of the Anglo-Jewish community in the 1880s and 90s.

Stern continually propagated the modernising, 'beautifying' and above all, the Westernising of the

* See Glossary

conduct of the service in his synagogue. His aim and influence was to make the East London a 'model of decorous worship'. In effect, he saw these efforts as part of the movement for Jewish emancipation and in his day this was a matter of great concern and of much controversy. One of his innovations was the introduction of a mixed choir at his synagogue – he claimed that it enabled young Jewish men and women to meet and encouraged marriage within the community. The mixed choir was, incidentally, one of the main factors leading to the formation of the Stepney Orthodox Synagogue (also in Stepney Green). This newer synagogue saw itself as a 'fortress' against 'laxity' and radical ideas – rather as the Machzike Hadath in Fournier Street stood to resist the influence of the Anglicised Judaism of the West End Synagogues.

The Great War seemed to bring out the Rev. Stern's patriotism and he lost no opportunity to denounce from the pulpit any able-bodied man who did not join His Majesty's Armed Forces and fight for his country.

To do him justice, one must bear in mind that over his long Ministry, he did a great deal to promote social welfare for the poor. He organised schemes for slum clearance and new housing. He helped the unemployed to gain new manual skills and was on numerous committees of education. He was the principal founder of the Committee of Workers among the Jewish Poor (in 1903 he was its first chairman) and President of the Stepney Jewish Lads' Club. The human misery and social ills of Stepney deeply affected him and he did not spare himself in practical ways to help the underprivileged. He became in a real sense the principal spokesman of the London Jewish world to the world of East London and was seen by the East End Jews as their means of communication with that wider world.

East London Synagogue, Rectory Square, Stepney Green

When he was honoured with the CBE in 1929, *The Times* wrote: 'But for the wisdom, sympathy and unflagging courage of men like ... J.F. Stern, the process of absorbing and digesting that great influx of foreign Jews would have caused a far more serious social upheaval than, in fact, it did'.

Even in death he was an innovator: he was cremated at Golders Green. Although he had been the Minister of a Congregation of the United Synagogue, it was the Rabbi of the West London Reform Synagogue who officiated at the service where it was announced that his ashes were to be interred in Palestine. He made a notable contribution to the concept of the Rabbi as Minister of his congregation and he remains a fascinating oddity: an East End Rabbi whose heart was in the Anglicised world of the West End.

The East London Synagogue, especially in the years between 1880 and 1914 when Stern was the Minister, made it possible for the foreign-born Jewish immigrants to belong to the mainstream United Synagogue movement and remain in the East End. They did not want to join the *shtieblach* nor could they afford to belong to the established congregations of the City of London: they would not have felt comfortable in the large city synagogues.

Behind the grim grey-brick Victorian facade the synagogue had a splendid Byzantine interior with ornate gilded columns and arches round the Ark. The central *bimah* had four large brass candelabra and there was a carved mahogany pulpit. It also preserved undamaged its original stained-glass windows despite extensive bombing of Stepney during the Second World War.

The East London, one of the oldest United Synagogue buildings, was sold at the end of 1987 to a property developer. The congregation of about 600 moved to a community centre next door where services are held. The closure of this historic building aroused protests from East End Jews and this plea from Dr Sharman Kadish:

> The interior of this cathedral synagogue – one of the few remaining – features skilful woodcarving, brasswork, brilliant William Morris-style mosaics and leaded stained glass. Immediate steps should be taken to ensure that this synagogue is made a listed building and protected from the grasp of property developers.[8]

But it was too late. The synagogue has since suffered extensive damage from fire, flood, vandalism and theft.

The Congregation of Jacob

This East End *shul* in Commercial Road, Stepney, is built in the traditional style of the Orthodox Federation type of synagogue and kept alive by the devotion of two elderly brothers, Israel and Morris Lixenberg. Israel is the President and Morris the Vice-President, who conducts the service on Friday evenings and on Sabbath mornings. Only about twelve to eighteen elderly people attend the weekly services, but the synagogue is full on the High Holydays. The congregation of about 250 members are mostly pensioners on low incomes who look forward to the distribution of the popular Chanukah Club run by the Treasurer, Israel Lixenberg.

The Congregation of Jacob was established in 1904 when Jewish immigrants from Eastern Europe were still arriving in large numbers. The synagogue is very near the London Docks and one of the first familiar places the new immigrants could go after landing in London. The present synagogue was built in 1920; it is welcoming although a bit shabby. The central *bimah* is made of mahogany and still highly polished; the Ark has the usual blue velvet curtain and above it the traditional pair of gilt lions supporting the tablet of the Ten Commandments. The central skylight gives a feeling of space in the narrow interior. Anyone who attends the services here feels involved and included. The warmth and intimacy are very comforting, and it is no wonder this synagogue inspires loyalty and devotion.

The congregation is affiliated to the Federation of Synagogues but self-supporting and proud of its financial independence.

The Wlodowa Synagogue

The sole survivor of the Jewish working-men's synagogues, the Wlodowa was originally established in Spital Square in 1901. It came to Cheshire Street when two congregations amalgamated in 1910: the United Workmen's Synagogue (mainly cabinet-makers) and the Hare Street Synagogue. Sadly, the beautiful interior in wood, all made by the cabinet-makers of the congregation, is no more. Until recently the synagogue was in use, although very bare and poorly furnished. The Ladies' Gallery was saved when the small *shul* was reconsecrated after falling into disuse in the years following the Second World War. No one entered the synagogue for seven years, and when the building was re-opened, the fine interior was in ruins; even the floor had to be concreted to make it safe. So few people used

Congregation of Jacob, Commercial Road, E1

The Wlodowa Synagogue, Cheshire Street, E2

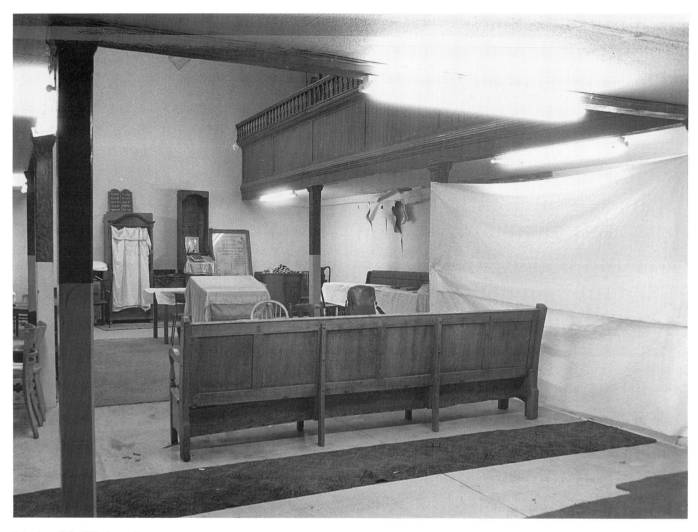

Interior of the Wlodowa Synagogue

it in its last years that only a sheet divided the men from the women during services. The guardian of the *shul* was Stanley Kinn, whose name appropriately derives from 'Kinnamann', meaning a woodworker in the Temple. Mr Kinn is a member of the Lubavich (a Chasidic community) and lives in Stamford Hill.

This historic synagogue was forced to close in 1987 because of fears about its safety; in fact, it had a dangerous structure notice served on it. According to a report in the *Jewish Chronicle* (1 January 1988) the remaining members of the synagogue decided that a new Wlodowa was not needed in the East End, and that it should move to Cliftonville, the 'posh' end of Margate. Thus the independent Wlodowa sold its site in Bethnal Green for redevelopment and bought an 18-bedroom hotel on the sea-front at Cliftonville. When the newly kosher hotel opens after refurbishment, the 160–80 elderly synagogue members will be able to enjoy communal weekends, Sabbath Services and High Holy-

day Festivals at the seaside. The kosher hotel will also provide Services for youth groups and Friendship Clubs for other congregations in the Jewish community.

The Wlodowa lives again; it must be the only East End Synagogue to have gone to sea.

Princelet Street Synagogue

An historic East End synagogue which was abandoned in 1983, the Princelet Street Synagogue has now been restored as a museum by the Heritage Centre. It is dedicated to the immigrants of the district: the Huguenots, the Jews and the Bengalis. The house at Number 19, Princes Street was built in 1718 by Samuel Worrall, the master carpenter for the architect, Nicholas Hawksmoor. He also built Worrall House in Princelet

Princelet Street Synagogue, Princes Street, E1

The Hackney Synagogue (interior)

Street, a fine specimen of its period, lovingly renovated under the guidance of the Spitalfields Trust. In 1862, No 19 became a synagogue when the building was extended over the garden of the house which had belonged to a Huguenot silk-weaver. The congregation had occupied a house in Fashion Street (Stepney) before they moved to Princelet Street where they were known as the United Friends' Synagogue.

An unusual form of charity was introduced at the Princelet Street Synagogue in 1888 in the form of a reduced marriage fee to poor brides. Four brides were granted the Israelite Marriage Portion Society's endowment of ten guineas (£10.10s.) and free marriage fees. Such generosity was unacceptable to the Rev. J.F. Stern, the very Anglo-Jewish Minister of the East London Synagogue, who had publicly spoken against 'young and Improvident marriages'.

The congregation mainly consisted of poor Jews who worked in the tailoring and garment trade, and the synagogue itself is small and simple. Whether decked with flowers for a festival (see page 59) or in its everyday furnishings – brass candelabra, blue velvet curtains over the Ark – it has a modest beauty which, fortunately, can still be seen.

The Hackney Synagogue, Brenthouse Road, E9

This large synagogue, once one of the major constituents of the United Synagogue, was built in 1896 and consecrated in 1897. Designed by Delissa Joseph, it was considered so good an example of the period that a drawing of the building was displayed at the Royal Academy in the year of its construction.

The spacious interior has the *bimah* set well back leaving plenty of room in front of the carpeted steps leading up to the Ark. For wedding ceremonies the *chupa* (canopy) is garlanded and set up in this space in front of the Ark. White marble columns support the Ladies' Galleries and add to the impression of dignity and space. It all serves to emphasise the incongruity of a place that no longer fits its surrounding district. During the inter-war period (1919–39) Hackney became a bustling, thriving district, full of the vitality of Jewish commercial and residential life. For many East Enders it was the first step to a better life and a move up in the world from the poorer parts of Stepney and Mile End. In those years the Hackney Synagogue grew at a great rate; it was enlarged to seat a thousand members when it amalgamated with the Richmond Synagogue in 1936.

The synagogue now seems isolated in a shabby, run-down neighbourhood. The interior is still well-kept, and the Wardens take time and trouble to show visitors their fine synagogue with pride and devotion. Until recently there were still more than 700 members of the congregation but fewer than half of them live in Hackney or nearby districts. These long-standing members for the most part maintain their connection for sentimental reasons, or very often they wish to be buried in the cemetery connected with their synagogue. (The historic Hackney Cemetery, opened in 1788, originally belonged to the Hambro' Synagogue but was closed to burials in 1886.) Sadly for the future, there are few young members of the congregation and no children who would require religious education. The 'children' have all moved away from Hackney.

Yavneh Synagogue

This fine traditional synagogue in Ainsworth Road, Hackney, like so many in the East End, has almost lost its *raison d'être*. The congregation was first established in 1904, originally in a stable, and was known as the North East London Beth Hamidrash. During the inter-war years, the district became a Jewish centre and the congregation grew rapidly. The charming early Victorian building was acquired in 1929 and completed in 1930. The interior is both handsome and well proportioned in a solid traditional lay-out. The Yavneh is a Constituent of the Federation of Synagogues.

On the occasion of the 75th anniversary of the founding of the Yavneh (in 1979) an old member of the congregation (Mr Charles Brooke) wrote a moving plea for the preservation of what he described as 'this great synagogue'. As a child he had been taken to the synagogue every Friday evening and all day on the Sabbath, and he went on to describe 'the rows of wooden forms, the Ark of the Law filled with the Sifrei Torah and the "Gallery" which consisted of a large square cordoned off and lace curtains at the top, which the ladies could lift to see what was going on . . . I used to go to learn Gemorra every Saturday afternoon with the Rabbonim and to my delight at the end of the session was rewarded with schmultz herring and beer, which in those days was really something'.

The Yavneh

The Yavneh (interior)

Great Garden Street Synagogue

Great Garden Street Synagogue

Eating Kosher food and being an Orthodox Jew are inseparable. 'Eating and drinking, said the rabbis, are religious acts for during them, man partakes of God's bounty'. What could be more fitting, therefore, than a synagogue building that houses a kosher restaurant?

Great Garden Street is a traditional East End synagogue near Whitechapel, still in its original building in Greatorex Street, E1. It was established nearly a century ago (in 1894), and although much of the surrounding district was bombed in the blitz, the *shul* escaped damage. The President of the synagogue was Morris Kasler and the hall which houses the Kosher Luncheon Club is named after him. It continues a tradition of Jewish soup kitchens and eating houses set up in the nineteenth century to cater for the needs of the East European Jews, who often arrived in East London with little more than the clothes they were wearing. These kosher 'kitchens' provided warmth, regional dishes and a *heimish* (homely and friendly) atmosphere for the newly arrived immigrants.

By the beginning of the Second World War, these simple eating-places had disappeared. The refugees they had served could afford better meals in their own homes. To keep the tradition alive in the 1960s two far-sighted members of the synagogue – Mr Lederman and Mr Goldman – set up the Kosher Luncheon Club with the blessing of the Federation of Synagogues. The menu offers bean and barley, tomato and rice soups but the speciality is fish – fried, grilled or steamed – with *latkes* (potato pancakes) and on Fridays delicious minced salmon cutlets. It is less frenetic (and a bit cheaper) than Bloom's in Whitechapel. You don't have to be Jewish to enjoy lunch at this old-fashioned fish and dairy restaurant. Usually it is full of local Muslims, Jewish tourists and non-Jewish customers (who work in the district) having a kosher lunch served by friendly, attentive waitresses.

The synagogue itself is well worth a visit. The semi-cupola above the Ark is supported by blue columns on either side and adds a Moorish note to the interior. The central *bimah* is surrounded by attractive globe lamps; the wooden balustrades of the ladies' galleries contribute to the late Victorian charm of the synagogue.

Notes

1. Nicholas Pevsner, *The Buildings of England* (Harmondsworth: Penguin, p.181.
2. Cecil Roth, *History of the Great Synagogue* (London: Edward Goldston, 1950).
3. Rev. John Entick, *New and Historical Survey of London*.
4. Roth, *History of the Great Synagogue*, p.173:
   At the time of her great benefaction to the Great Synagogue, Judith Levy was an old woman of eighty-four. But she lived on, more and more shrivelled, more and more eccentric, long after this. It was on January 18th, 1803, that the Queen of Richmond Green died at her mansion in Albermarle Street, Piccadilly. She was buried two days after in the ground which her father-in-law had acquired in 1697 and which her father had enlarged in 1748, between the husband and the son whom she had survived by upwards of half a century.
5. Edward Jamilly, 'Synagogue Art and Architecture' in Salmond S. Levin (ed.), *A Century of Anglo-Jewish Life* (London: United Synagogue, 1971), p.76.
6. Beatrice Potter, 'The Jews of London', Ch.3 in Charles Booth (ed.), *Life and Labour of the People* (London, 1892).
7. Israel Finestein, 'Joseph Frederick Stern, 1865–1934: Aspects of a Gifted Anomaly', in Aubrey Newman (ed.), *The Jewish East End, 1840–1939* (London: The Jewish Historical Society of England, 1981), pp.75–98.
8. Dr Sharman Kadish, 'Time for some imagination in the East End', letter in the *Jewish Chronicle*, 18 December 1987. See also 'Sadness at Synagogue Sell-off' in the *East London Advertiser* of the same date.

4

The West End Synagogues

The Western Synagogue

Westminster in the eighteenth century was a very different place from the overcrowded City of London and in particular the East End with its unpaved streets and lack of sanitation. The Jews of the City and the East End were either very wealthy or very poor, and life for the poor in Georgian England was 'nasty, brutish and short' indeed. The City of Westminster was less congested, had more green, open space and better air to breathe and was more fashionable; thus it attracted the wealthy with money to spend on clothes and jewellery. The enlightened authorities of Westminster passed the Westminster Paving Act at about the same time as a small colony of Jews settled there and established their small *chevra*-cum-synagogue. The Paving Commission greatly hastened the growth of Westminster and improved not only its pavements but its roads, drainage and sewage. The changes attracted a handful of Jews from the City of London and made Westminster 'a metropolis that is the admiration of all Europe and far exceeds anything of its kind in the modern world'.

In 1761 in Great Pulteney Street, Westminster, a small group of Jewish merchants, together with some shopkeepers and artisans, met in the home of Wolf Liepman, 'a Gentleman from St. Petersburg' where apparently he had been a Counsellor to the Czar of all the Russias. He lived in Berlin and Vienna before settling in London; for some years he maintained at his own expense a *minyan** which evolved into 'the Holy Congregation of the Keneseth Israel of Westminster in London'. The original congregation was called 'Hebra Kaddisha Shel Gemillith Hassadim, Westminster', a combination of Friendly Society, synagogue and burial society.

* See Glossary

Its first home was in Denmark Court (off the Strand) in the years between 1765 and 1826 (although a secessionist movement established a rival congregation in Brewer Street and later in Maiden Lane). In 1826 the Westminster Synagogue moved and re-established itself at St. Alban's Place in the Haymarket, right in the heart of the West End. It became a splendid temple after some rebuilding and refurbishing in the years between 1826 and 1832 when it changed its name officially to 'The Western Synagogue'. The *minyan* that began in Wolf Liepman's house had become one of the great synagogues of London and had among its congregation the wealthiest London Jews – many of the most successful City businessmen had left the synagogues of the 'Square Mile' to join the Western. The ceremony of Consecration was reported in the *Morning Post* of 5 September 1836 and clearly shows how important this synagogue and its congregation had become:

> The imposing ceremony of consecration according to the Jewish rites took place at the Synagogue in St. Alban's Place. The present appearance of the chapel is extremely beautiful ... The building is remarkable for its elegance and chasteness ... It is constructed of white marble, richly decorated with gold and supported on each side by two handsome coloured pillars of beautiful workmanship. The veil of the Ark is composed of rich white silk and the doors of highly polished oak ... At 6 o'clock the usual Afternoon Service commenced, after which, and an introductory symphony by a full band, the Chief Rabbi of England, a very aged and venerable-looking man, the Wardens and other Officers of the Congregation brought into the Synagogue the sacred Scrolls of the Law. The Synagogue was considerably crowded throughout the ceremony which lasted several hours.

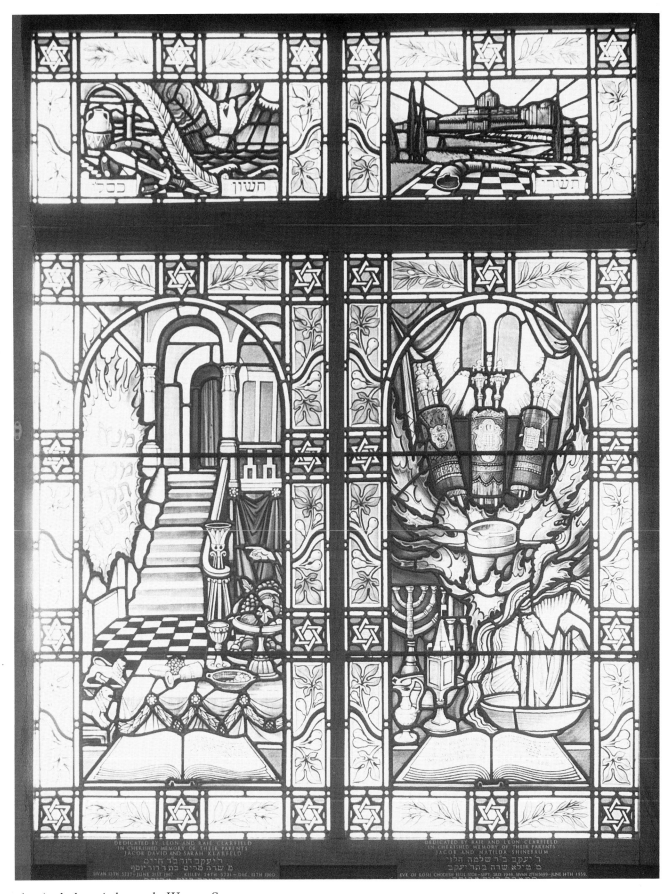

A stained-glass window at the Western Synagogue

By the 1880s, the Western included many notable figures in Anglo-Jewry: Sir Samuel Montagu, MP (Lord Swaythling); Sir Stuart Samuel, MP; Viscount Stern; Lady Battersea; Hannah de Rothschild; and Lady Rosebery, wife of the fifth Earl who became Prime Minister.

Yet in spite of its respectability and standing, the Western was never narrow in its Orthodoxy and developed a tolerant attitude to less conformist congregations. It maintained good relations with the Reform Movement and was one of the few synagogues that refused to read the proclamation banning the Reform Synagogue of British Jews when it was established as the West London Synagogue in 1840. The Western Congregation was therefore regarded as having some sympathy with the Reform Movement, and it certainly tended to attract some prominent Anglo-Jewish families like the Rothschilds, Goldsmids and Waleys who wanted some changes in the official Orthodox synagogues but were not willing to break away and join the Reform Movement.

The Western remained at St. Alban's Place until 1914 when, after nearly a century in the City of Westminster, it had to set up a new home in the Borough of Holborn. The old building had to be demolished and the congregation decided to erect a new building for a larger congregation, in Alfred Place, off Tottenham Court Road.

The First World War started soon after this move and delayed the completion of the Alfred Place synagogue for some years. The foundation was laid in June 1915 and gradually the Western began to occupy and use its new 'permanent' home in Alfred Place. However, like the archetypal Wandering Jew, the Western was forced to move again as a result of a direct hit during a bombing raid in 1941.

The Western came to its ninth and final home, in Crawford Place in 1957. The building, previously a Nonconformist chapel, was enlarged to provide adequate classrooms, a lecture hall, a library and museum and a large meeting-cum-banqueting hall. The exterior is modern and rather severe, but the interior has dignity and warmth. Numerous stained-glass windows add to the colour and the pleasing aspect of the interior.

The Western's traditional tolerance is exemplified in the policy of its cemetery in Edmonton. This cemetery, which opened its gates in 1884, has served as a burial ground for many congregations of widely divergent Jewish views. It has given burial facilities to synagogues of the Federation as well as other synagogues in North and South-East London and in more recent times to communities as different as the Adath-Israel and the Bernard Baron Settlement. Through its cemetery the Western Synagogue has indeed offered 'an acre of peace' and helped to reconcile Jews whose views kept them apart in life.

In May 1991 the historic Western was amalgamated with the Marble Arch Synagogue in Great Cumberland Place.

The Marble Arch Synagogue

This large, opulent synagogue is the newest of the 'magnificent seven' in the West End. Behind the discreet, curved neo-Georgian facade of Great Cumberland Place, the Marble Arch Synagogue can accommodate a thousand people as well as a small number of worshippers in the Mintz Beth Hamidrash. (The small synagogue is inside the main building on the first floor, where morning and evening services are held every weekday.) Almost next door to the Cumberland Hotel, the synagogue is very conveniently situated for overseas visitors. Rabbi Jonathan Sacks* once remarked, 'When I look down from the pulpit on a Shabbat morning I invariably see a bevy of unfamiliar faces. Although, one Shabbat recently, I was able to welcome the American conductor, Leonard Bernstein.'

For the United Synagogue, the Marble Arch was intended to replace the Great Synagogue in the City of London, which had been destroyed in an air-raid in 1941. It was designed by T.P. Bennett and Son, a successful non-Jewish firm of commercial architects, in 1962 as part of the Great Cumberland Place scheme. Like the new St. John's Wood Synagogue, also designed by Bennett and Son, it was expensive: costing more than a quarter of a million pounds.

Architecturally, it does little to replace the Great Synagogue. Behind the imitation Georgian-cum-Regency colonnade, the congregation has a 'modern' comfortable interior which can only be described as eclectic – modern lighting and streamlined Ark with the traditional lay-out of central *bimah* and a high Ladies' Gallery on three sides.

The Marble Arch Synagogue is not in any sense a new Great Synagogue. It probably was not possible for any new religious building to take the special place of the first Ashkenazi synagogue in Britain. Yet one cannot help feeling that a great opportunity was missed. Marble Arch could have inspired some young (or old)

* Now the Chief Rabbi

Marble Arch Synagogue: inside the Ark (Scrolls of the Law)

Consecration of the new Central Synagogue, 1870

Anglo-Jewish architect to produce a strikingly modern design which could have stood comparison with the Jewish cathedrals of the past. Instead, we have another bland compromise which has become a fashionable place for weddings (usually with the reception held in the adjacent King David Suite), and a convenient place for Jewish overseas visitors who wish to go to a service in the West End.

The Central Synagogue

The Central Synagogue in its splendid Victorian building in Great Portland Street became one of the great cathedrals of Anglo-Jewry and remained so until the Second World War. 'Traditional lay-out with central bimah, Moorish in detail. Gothic in feeling – it

had a soaring vaulted nave – and employed cast-iron columns. It cost £24,000 and seated eight hundred and sixty, the largest synagogue yet.'[1] Designed by N.S. Joseph, it was erected in 1869–70. On 10 May 1941 this fine building was destroyed by bombs during an air-raid.

Originally, the Central was set up in 1848 as an annexe of the Great Synagogue to offset the rival attractions of the West London Reform, the only other synagogue in the West End. A warehouse was acquired in the 1850s and reconstructed; it was consecrated in 1855 and the Central Synagogue came into being. For its first 25 years, the Central existed only as an offshoot of the Great Synagogue and could not celebrate marriages or appoint its own officers. By the end of the 1860s, it had grown to such an extent that it needed

The Central Synagogue, 1870

The Marriage of Mr Leopold de Rothschild and Mademoiselle Marie Perugia in the Central Synagogue

The New Central Synagogue (1958), Great Portland Street, W1

a new larger permanent building and, moreover, its congregation wanted to emerge from the shadow of the Great. In April 1870, the new building was consecrated by the Chief Rabbi, and the Ark was opened by Sir Moses Montefiore, then 85 years of age. It was very much a grand Anglo-Jewish 'establishment' occasion and re-launched the Central as the leading synagogue in the West End for the wealthy upper-crust Jew. Sir Anthony de Rothschild was one of the first Wardens, and it was fashionable for the Rothschilds to hold their weddings at the Central. In July 1871, Dom Pedro II, the Emperor of Brazil, visited the synagogue and a prayer book and an illuminated address were presented to him. *The Times* reported the event in great detail on its first page:

> The visit of the Emperor to the Central Synagogue is the first that has been paid in this country by a reigning Sovereign to a synagogue during Divine Service. We may add that His Majesty is versed in the Hebrew language and was consequently able to read and understand the Service.

After the loss of the old Central in the Second World War, the congregation kept together by holding services at the Academy of Music in Marylebone Road and at Woburn House. The new Central Synagogue took two years to build and was completed in 1958. A modern building, supposedly based on 'Venetian baroque', it has a cantilever structure with stained-glass windows depicting Jewish festivals. It is again a large synagogue which seats more than 500 on the ground-floor and 400 in the Ladies' Gallery; below the synagogue there is a spacious Assembly Hall. The Consecration of the new Central took place in March 1958; and the service was conducted by the Chief Rabbi, Dr Israel Brodie, and by Rabbi Cyril Shine.

Up to the end of the 1960s, the Central and its modern home continued to attract members and remained pre-eminent among the Orthodox West End synagogues. Since then its membership and its influence have declined, although it still has a scattered congregation of about 700 families – Jews with country homes and flats in town. Its long-term future is now uncertain, although it is still viable and a 'going concern'.

The West London Synagogue

The West London Synagogue of British Jews in Upper Berkeley Street, W1 is not only an outstanding example of synagogue architecture but the most important temple of the Reform Movement in Great Britain. The magnificent interior is surprising if one is not aware of the origins of the Reform Synagogue in this country. The strong Moorish influence in the great arches of the interior and cupola above the Ark are eloquent reminders of the Sephardic background of the founding fathers of the synagogue and of the links with the Spanish and Portuguese Synagogue from which they broke away.

The West London Synagogue was established in Upper Berkeley Street in 1870, but the congregation had already been in existence since 1840. Most of the founders were members of Bevis Marks, the venerable Sephardic synagogue in the City. Many of the Anglo-Jewish members felt that the ways of Bevis Marks were remote from their daily lives in England. The 'gabbling of the Hebrew prayers' in the Orthodox Ashkenazi Synagogue in Duke's Place was equally unappealing, and they decided in 1840 to set up a place of worship for Jews in this country, whatever their origin, where they could perform a revised form of worship. In 1842 the first synagogue of the Reform Movement was consecrated in modest premises in Bruton Street, St. Pancras, a week after the congregation had been excommunicated by both the Ashkenazi and the Sephardic authorities. The reformers were not even permitted burial in a Jewish cemetery and could not celebrate marriages in their synagogue under the New Acts of Parliament because the President of the Board of Deputies, Sir Moses Montefiore, refused 'to consider the place of worship in Bruton Street to be a Synagogue', even though his brother was one of the founders.

But the congregation grew and flourished, until by 1849 the little synagogue in Bruton Street was too small, and they moved to larger premises in Margaret Street, Cavendish Square.

In 1866 they acquired the site in Berkeley Street and sufficient funds to appoint the architects, Davis and Emanuel, to design the building and also to obtain tenders for an organ. The new synagogue was completed in 1870. The main difference between the building then and as it is now is that the reading desk was in the centre. It was moved to the east side (thus spoiling the impressive sweep of the steps to the Ark) at the end of the century.

The Ark is notable for its open grille work through which the Sifrei Torah (the Scrolls of the Torah) can be seen by most members of the congregation throughout the services. In front of the Ark is a specially-designed 'Moorish' *ner tamid* (everlasting light) suspended on a chain from the high domed ceiling. The *chanukiah*

The West London Synagogue, Upper Berkeley Street, W1

West London Synagogue: Ordination Service of Rabbis

(candelabrum with nine branches) is made of brass and was specially designed for the congregation in 1848. Both the *ner tamid* and the *chanukiah* are run on oil, but whereas the *ner tamid* is constantly in use, of course, the candelabrum is only used for the eight days of Chanukah.

The organ behind the Ark was constructed in 1870 by the same firm that built the one in the Royal Albert Hall. The choir is accommodated near the organ behind the Ark – the choir loft has been extended and a loudspeaker system installed to improve the acoustics of the building. Most of the windows are of stained glass and decorated with abstract patterns and images of trees and fruit. The dome has a particularly fine window featuring the Star of David.

The West London, perhaps the most beautiful of the Victorian synagogues, continues to flourish with a large congregation (about 2,500 families) led by three Rabbis: the well-known Dr Hugo Gryn, Mrs Jacqueline Tabick and Rabbi R. Shafritz. It has come a long way from its origins as a breakaway group who suffered excommunication and the abuse of the Orthodox. It is eminently respectable and in its own way, firmly traditional. By the year 1892, when it held its Jubilee Service to celebrate the fiftieth anniversary of its foundation, it was fully recognised as an important Anglo-Jewish institution.

The New West End Synagogue

If one had to choose one synagogue that symbolised successful Anglicised Jewry of the late Victorian and Edwardian period, then the New West End in St. Petersburgh Place, Bayswater, would be the obvious choice. In the middle of the last century, prosperous Jewish families moved into the area north of Hyde Park. The Bayswater Synagogue opened in Chichester Place in 1863, but proved too small for the growing community. It was decided to found a new synagogue within easier walking distance (for the Sabbath) in the very smart residential district near Kensington Gardens. The new congregation (like the older Bayswater Synagogue) became a part of the United Synagogue in 1879.

The building is a curious mixture of Gothic and Moorish features, which achieves a certain splendour in the interior. It is a listed building and is certainly a fine example of an Anglo-Jewish 'cathedral' of the nineteenth century. Among the special features of the interior are the horseshoe-shaped arches, reminiscent of the synagogues of mediaeval Moorish Spain, the rose windows which are Romanesque, and the Byzantine cupolas above the Ark. The Ark curtain was originally an eighteenth-century Spanish portière (presented by

Sir Joseph Duveen), but the present one was woven by the Royal School of Needlework.

The Rabbis of the New West End have been outstanding ministers and Jewish scholars from the first, Simeon Singer, to the more recent and controversial figure of Rabbi Dr Louis Jacobs (now the Minister of the New London Synagogue in St. John's Wood). The Rev. Singer (1846–1906) was a magnificent preacher and was described as 'the ideal of an Anglo-Jewish Minister'. However, he spoke for the Anglo-Jewish Establishment when he addressed the congregation on Rosh Hashanah in 1888, among whom were a considerable number of 'our Polish brethren'. He admonished the East European Jews in these words: 'Get rid as quickly as you can of those unpleasant pecularities of manners, habits and speech which are said to mark some Jews without distinguishing them, and which are apt to bring shame on all Jews'. His name became a household word among English-speaking Jews as he edited and translated the Authorised Daily Prayer Book which became known as 'Singer's Prayer Book'. He left his mark on the building by selecting the Hebrew texts, mainly from the Psalms, whose golden letters decorate the walls and front of the galleries in imitation of those at the thirteenth-century Abulafia Synagogue in Toledo.

Rabbi Jacobs held the office of Minister from 1954 to 1960, and the question of his re-appointment in the early 1960s (after a period at Jews' College) led not only to a split in the congregation and the departure of many members but to a major public dispute for the United Synagogue. The 'Jacobs affair' was partly theological and partly internal politics, involving the rights of a congregation to defy the Chief Rabbi. The controversy was taken up by the national Press and became a *cause célèbre* for the Anglo-Jewish community.

The New West End certainly suffered a dramatic loss of members as a result of the Chief Rabbi's refusal to authorise the re-appointment of Rabbi Jacobs in 1964. Rabbi Nemeth was appointed in 1965, and the synagogue recovered from the damage inflicted by the 'Jacobs Affair'. Until recently the New West End was in decline owing to the movement of its members to other parts of London. Bayswater and Notting Hill had changed and the districts no longer suited the wealthy, fashionable Jews who used to constitute the majority of the congregation. However, there are signs of revival since the Bayswater Synagogue closed, as some of its members have joined the New West End and its present membership of about 350 includes new members from the Holland Park area into which young Jewish couples have been moving.

The New West End Synagogue, Bayswater (interior)

The New West End Synagogue
(exterior)

The West Central Synagogue

A synagogue founded and led by a woman must be unique in such a male-dominated religion. The woman was, of course, a rare and remarkable person: Lily Montagu, daughter of the strictly Orthodox Sir Samuel Montagu, not only created the West Central Synagogue, but helped to form a Movement, the Union of Liberal and Progressive Synagogues. In 1893, Lily and her sister, Marian, organised a Bible class in Bloomsbury from which they developed the West Central Jewish Girls' Club. All the Club meetings featured Jewish prayers which enabled Lily Montagu to introduce a new approach to Judaism with more appeal to young women than the traditional form of worship. In 1899, she expressed the urgent need for Judaism to be presented so that it would give meaning and guidance to those who were being lost to Jewish religious teaching. An article she wrote for the *Jewish Quarterly Review* aroused the interest of many prominent Jews and, with their help, Lily Montagu and C.G. Montefiore formed the Jewish Religious Union in 1902. The JRU held services in an hotel in Marylebone where for the first time many of the prayers were in English.

The district north of Soho, the West Central area, had become 'an East End in the West End', especially after the First World War. Jewish shops and restaurants, a largely Jewish market, tailors' workshops and small factories manufacturing ladies' garments but the only local synagogues were the traditionally Orthodox and rather grand synagogues like the Central in Great Portland Street. In this working-class Jewish neighbourhood, the West Central Section of the Jewish Religious Union had members but little money – most of the congregation were women followers of the Montagu sisters. Lacking not only money but also men, they could not officially form a congregation, nor could they afford to appoint a minister. Services were mainly conducted by Lily Montagu until 1928 when the Liberal Jewish Synagogue appointed Rabbi Solomon Starrels to serve as Minister.

The first service of the West Central Synagogue took place in September 1928. Since then regular services have been held that include choral and organ music with prayers in Hebrew and in English. From the beginning women have played an important part in the services and in running the synagogue. A special feature is the Saturday afternoon service, a practice which dates back to the early days of the congregation when most of the members were women who worked five and a half days a week, including Saturday morning. (The Sabbath service on Saturday afternoon originally began in the Jewish Religious Union.) Even the annual general meetings of the Congregation were unusual: they used to be held in the open air after a special service, followed by tea in the garden of the home of another of Lily Montagu's sisters, the Hon. Mrs Netta Franklin.

Lily Montagu was given the title of Lay Minister by the Union of Liberal and Progressive Synagogues in 1943. She was the first woman to be a Jewish Minister in Great Britain and conducted services in a hat and gown, but without a *talluth*. In addition to her religious and social work, she served for many years as a magistrate in St. Pancras and was one of the first women to become a Justice of the Peace. Those who knew this remarkable woman would agree with Rabbi Edgar who wrote, 'Lily Montagu was one of the outstanding Jewish religious personalities of our time'.[2]

In 1937 she was awarded the OBE for her outstanding social work, and she became a CBE in 1955 for her services to Jewish organisations. She died in 1963 in her 90th year.

Overshadowed by the Post Office Tower, the plain brick building in Whitfield Street which houses the synagogue was given to the Union of Liberal and Progressive Synagogues for use as their headquarters on condition that the congregation would continue to have use of it for their services and other activities. The building also houses the European Board of the World Union for Progressive Judaism. In 1970, the building was appropriately renamed the Montagu Centre.

Lily Montagu, Minister of the West Central Synagogue

The Westminster Synagogue: the barrel-vaulted ceiling of the entrance hall at Kent House

The Westminster Synagogue

A stately Victorian mansion, Kent House, in Rutland Gardens, Knightsbridge, has been the home of the Westminster Synagogue since 1960. The original house was rented and lived in by Edward, Duke of Kent (the fourth son of George III and father of Queen Victoria), who enlarged it and named it after his own title. In 1870 the old mansion was pulled down and the present Kent House built on the same foundations. Celia Noble, grand-daughter of the great engineer, Isambard Kingdom Brunel, created a notable salon in the drawing-rooms of the house using the talents of the Spanish artist, J.M. Sert. The musical soirées became celebrated; famous musicians performed here, among whom were the cellist Suggia, Dame Myra Hess, Joachim and Sir Donald Tovey. Sarah Bernhardt, Diaghilev and members of his famous ballet company were often entertained at Kent House.

The Westminster Synagogue began as the New London Jewish Congregation. A small group of former members had broken away from the West London Synagogue over the enforced retirement of Rabbi Harold Reinhardt, the Senior Minister. These loyal followers negotiated the purchase of Kent House as the home of a new independent synagogue to be led by Dr Reinhardt. He became the first Minister of the new congregation in 1957, although the first service in Kent House was not held until September 1960. Dr Reinhardt and his wife had a flat on the third floor above the synagogue, and he remained Rabbi of the Westminster until his death in 1969.

When the congregation acquired the house in 1960, it was in a sad state of neglect and disrepair. It had been taken over in 1940 as wartime offices and had not been used for many years after the war. The Westminster Congregation gradually restored the building and on 15 September 1963 the new synagogue was consecrated at a service attended by many representatives of the Anglo-Jewish community.

Kent House, now a centre of Jewish prayer and study, is unique in being the repository for more than 1,500 Sifrei Torah (Scrolls of Scripture). These Scrolls were saved from hundreds of Czechoslovak synagogues desecrated and ransacked by the Nazis. Since 1964 these priceless Scrolls have been kept in Kent House where they are being repaired and studied. About 500 of them have already been distributed to synagogues, Talmud Torah and other institutions in many countries. Kent House also contains an extensive library, a collection of synagogue vestments and ceremonial objects.

The Westminster is an independent synagogue within the Reform tradition. Rabbi Albert Friedlander has been the Minister of the congregation since 1971.

The West End Great Synagogue

Although Soho is still a district of 'foreigners', the West End Great in Dean Street has become more Anglicised as its congregation has become more settled. Its rival, the Central, in Great Portland Street was more 'established' in the days before the Second World War. One member of the Central Synagogue today recalls when her family belonged to the West End Great at the time of its home in Manette Street. The family's name is Mendoza and the great prize fighter, Daniel, was a direct relative. Mrs Mendoza's father was a barber and the family lived above the shop. She went to school at St. Peter's, just off Berwick Street. The Mendoza family found the synagogue in Manette Street much 'too foreign'. They were born in England, although the grandparents had come from Poland on her mother's side and from Germany on her father's side. The Mendozas transferred their membership to the Central Synagogue, which had a mixed congregation, but seemed to have many more well-established Anglo-Jewish families. The difference between the two synagogues certainly had to do with social class. Not only did the West End Great have more families of foreign origin but the majority were small traders who lived nearby or had shops or stalls in the Berwick Street Market.

Originally linked to the West End Talmud Torah, the congregation was established in 1880 at No 10, Green Court in Soho. About 100 children of Jewish families studied Hebrew and Judaism in the classes held in Green Court. The Jews of Soho were small shopkeepers, factory workers or just poor, newly arrived immigrants. They were mostly tailors or semi-skilled workers in the garment-making workshops – very different from the smart, affluent wholesalers in the fashion business still centred on Great Portland Street and Margaret Street. In 1915 a fund was set up to provide clothing and footwear for 'the Jewish poor in the district' and in 1918 a 'Distress and Loan Fund' was instituted to assist needy members of the congregation.

In 1910, the congregation amalgamated with the Bikkur Cholim Synagogue and took larger and better premises at 41 Brewer Street. In 1914 when the Great War started, the synagogue purchased a site for a burial ground in Streatham (in South London), which was consecrated in 1915. The West End Talmud Torah

The West End Great Synagogue, Dean Street

and Synagogue moved again in 1916 to a larger building in Manette Street (Soho), and was registered as a House of Worship authorised to solemnise weddings. The first marriage ceremony was performed in 1917 at a cost of £1.11s.6d, and the couple were presented with silver candlesticks to mark the occasion.

The congregation continued to grow after the First World War – in 1926 the Scala Theatre was used for the first time for the High Holyday Services to contain the greatly enlarged membership. The synagogue became a focal point for the Soho Jewish community during the 1920s and 1930s, and was especially active in promoting meetings to protest on behalf of persecuted Jews in Germany. The congregation acquired its home in Dean Street in 1941, but the building was damaged by bombs in the remaining years of the Second World War. It was re-opened after extensive repairs in 1950 and its second amalgamation with the Beth Hasepher, when it became known as the West End Great Syna-

gogue. The present building which is modern in the 'functional' style, was the result of a major re-building in 1960; the synagogue was re-opened and consecrated at 21 Dean Street when Rabbi M. Lew was inducted.

Today, the West End Great is part of a complex of Jewish social, cultural and political activities. The synagogue occupies the first two floors with a large banqueting hall and a smaller hall for meetings. On the top floor, the well-known Ben Uri Gallery exhibits paintings by Jewish artists and holds recitals and lectures. On another floor are the offices of the Labour Friends of Israel, the British Na'amat and the Boys' Town Jerusalem, a charitable organisation for orphans.

The West End Great still has a scattered membership of about 600, many of whom, wherever they live, keep up their membership more for the right to be buried at their cemetery in Streatham than for the religious or social activities the synagogue offers in this life.

Bayswater Synagogue (interior)

The Bayswater Synagogue

In September 1963 a headline in the *Jewish Chronicle* announced: 'THE BAYSWATER SYNAGOGUE TO BE DEMOLISHED'. Even the Minister of the synagogue, Rabbi Raymond Apple, was astonished to learn that the Greater London Council had decided that the site on which the synagogue had stood for a century was required for a motorway development. Within three years a famous synagogue had been destroyed.

When it celebrated its centenary (in 1963), the Bayswater Synagogue could claim 'the distinction of being the oldest Ashkenazi place of worship standing in London'.[3] It was one of the five founder synagogues that created the United Synagogue and had been known as 'the Chief Rabbi's synagogue'. It came into being at a time when the Jewish population of England was still small: in 1850 there were no more than 35,000–40,000 Jews in the whole of Britain, of whom about two-thirds lived in London. Yet this number was twice as many as there had been at the beginning of the century, without a corresponding growth in the number of synagogues. In 1800 there were only the four synagogues in the City: The Great, the Hambro' and the New for the Ashkenazi community and the Bevis Marks for the Sephardim. In the West End there were the Western and Maiden Lane Synagogues. In addition to these six, in Southwark the Borough Synagogue served a small community south of the Thames. Apart from these, there were various small congregations, mainly of Polish Jews, who managed to maintain their synagogues through connections with one or other of the major ones. By the middle of the nineteenth century the religious needs of the Jews of London were hardly being met. The London Jew and his family had already begun moving out of the traditional areas of Jewish settlement in the East side of the City. By 1860, Jews were living in Bloomsbury, Marylebone, Westminster and north of Hyde Park, in Bayswater.

The lack of synagogues in these parts of London caused great discontent. Jewish families had moved west and felt separated from the traditional centres of worship and the provision of teaching for their children. The situation was aggravated by the strict, even harsh attitude of the wardens of the older synagogues, the 'Jewish City Fathers', who had powers that can hardly be imagined today. If members of the synagogue could not walk from their homes to the City to attend the service on the Sabbath and proposed private worship in their own neighbourhoods, they were threatened with excommunication.

The foundation of the West London Synagogue of Reform Jews was partly a result of this unsatisfactory state of affairs, but it was not a solution for the majority who wanted to worship in the traditional Orthodox way. Most of the families in Bayswater and Maida Vale were not attracted to the Reform synagogue. In 1844 a change of Chief Rabbi opened the door to new solutions. Nathan Marcus Adler, unlike his predecessor, Solomon Hirschell, was actively in touch with his congregations, and within a short time, he urged the Great to establish a 'branch' near Oxford Circus. As a result, the Central Synagogue was created in 1855 (although it was not fully established until 1870). Chief Rabbi Adler encouraged the Jews living in Bayswater to set up their own synagogue and in 1860, the first meetings were held to decide where it was to be. The founders chose a site in Chichester Place (near the Harrow Road and the Paddington Canal), which was then a modern suburban street in a green and pleasant neighbourhood. The building was mainly the work of Edward Salomons of Manchester, although N. S. Joseph did contribute to the design.[4] The Bayswater Synagogue cost £15,000 to construct and accommodated 341 men on the ground floor and 334 women in the Ladies' Gallery. The Chief Rabbi laid the cornerstone of the new synagogue on 10 July 1862.

The synagogue was much admired and became a model for several synagogues in other countries. It was conceived as a permanent home for its congregation and for wider use as a cathedral synagogue. The building was formidably solid with Romanesque arches over the main entrance and upper windows. The interior was more successful: it had space, dignity and a restrained traditional unity of style. The parent synagogue, the Great, donated a number of ceremonial objects for the new synagogue, including some ritual silver of great beauty. The Scroll of the Torah was particularly splendid, adorned by golden bells made in Holland and with a green velvet mantle (made by Abrahams of Lisle Street, embroiderers to Queen Victoria).

From its earliest days, Bayswater was a special congregation. Many of its members were distinguished people and soon there was something of a cachet attached to belonging to this fine synagogue. It developed a reputation beyond its own area and attracted outstanding people in the social and religious life of London and in Europe. Among the many well-known Jews associated with Bayswater were two outstanding Rabbis: Hermann Adler and Hermann Gollancz. Dr Hermann Adler (the son of Nathan Marcus Adler) who became Chief Rabbi in 1891, began as Reader at the age of 25 at Bayswater. During his 27 years at the synagogue, he rarely conducted a service. He was always essentially a teacher: he preached and he supervised Hebrew classes. In his long career, he read and preached at many synagogues all over London. His magnetic personality inspired great devotion, especially, it seems among the women in the congregation. Although a considerable scholar, he had a nice sense of humour. At a banquet where he met Cardinal Newman, the Cardinal asked him, 'When are you going to eat ham, Dr Adler?' The Rabbi replied, 'At your wedding, Your Eminence.'

Hermann Adler was unusual in being a religious leader who was both Orthodox and enlightened with an original mind. His concern was to help the worshipper to pray with intelligence and understanding. Deeply religious and involved in practical social work, he was one of the leaders of the Society for the Prevention of Cruelty to Children. At his death in 1911, it was said that 'no man was more revered and beloved throughout Jewry'.[5]

The name Gollancz has long been associated with publishing, but one of the most distinguished members of the family was an outstanding Rabbi at the Bayswater synagogue. Hermann Gollancz was born in Bremen where his father was a Rabbi; he was brought to England as an infant of 18 months. He became an outstanding linguist – he spoke Hebrew as well as English – and was the first Jew to become a Doctor of Literature. Later in his academic career, he held the Professorial Chair of Hebrew at University College, London. A unique honour was bestowed on him towards the end of his active life in 1923 when he was knighted. Professor Sir Hermann Gollancz was the only Rabbi in England to have been honoured in this way. At the time, the Bishop of Birmingham wrote to him: 'I do not know any man who has done more in quiet work to develop a noble, religious citizenship than yourself. He was a moderate Zionist and an active worker in promoting Jewish–Christian friendship. One of his close friends was Dr John Clifford, the Baptist Pastor at the nearby Westbourne Park Chapel when Dr Gollancz was Minister at Bayswater. In his Jubilee sermon he proclaimed one of his maxims: 'Religion should not act as a barrier between man and man but rather be a medium for unity'.

After the Second World War, the district of Bayswater became shabby and sadly run-down, and the synagogue began to suffer a decline. In spite of the change in the district and the movement of upper-middle-class Jews to more attractive areas, its special place and its hold on its congregation enabled it to survive. It is all the more surprising that only three years after this famous synagogue celebrated its centenary, it was pulled down, with no provisions to re-establish the congregation elsewhere. In August 1966, photographs appeared in the *Jewish Chronicle* showing the bulldozers demolishing the synagogue, and the newspaper announced 'a piece of history disappears'.

Some of the congregation were no doubt sad that this historic synagogue had not only closed down but was being razed to the ground. Anglo-Jewry, however, did not protest loudly at this act of public road-building through a historic synagogue. The congregation did not march up and down the Bayswater Road or sit down in front of County Hall with banners denouncing the GLC. More recently there were stronger protests at the proposed destruction of the Hoover factory on the Western Avenue with the result that it was saved. (Incidentally, it was the same road that caused the destruction of the Bayswater.) The remarkable fact is that the demolition of the synagogue was allowed to happen with so little fuss.

Notes

1. Edward Jamilly, 'Synagogue Art and Architecture' in Salmond S. Levin (ed.), *A Century of Anglo-Jewish Life, 1870–1970* (London: United Synagogue, 1971).
2. Rabbi Dr Leslie I. Edgar, *In Memory of Lily Montagu* (Amsterdam: Polak and Van Gennep, 1967).
3. O.S. Phillips and H.A. Simons, *The History of the Bayswater Synagogue* (London, 1963).
4. Ibid.
5. Levin (ed.), *A Century of Anglo-Jewish Life*.

5

Synagogues in North London

Stamford Hill

Stamford Hill is the Mea Shearim,[1] the Chasidic heartland of London. Although there are a number of Adath synagogues and Chasidic communities in Golders Green and Hendon, Stamford Hill is the home and centre for the Chasidic Jew in London. Why Stamford Hill?

It has a long history of Jewish settlement; even in the eighteenth century wealthy Jewish families had taken up residence in Stamford Hill. The Goldsmids, Montefiores and Rothschilds had country mansions and estates when there were no more than 237 houses in the whole district. By the time Henry Mayhew had compiled his survey of London (1851), Stamford Hill was considered 'a high class area' where 'a wealthy Jew millionaire merchant, stock-jobber or broker resides – in a villa in Regent's Park, a mansion near the Duke of Wellington's in Piccadilly or a house and grounds at Stamford Hill'.[2] The district has been through many phases of social change: from an upper-class country retreat for the Jewish rich in the late eighteenth and early nineteenth centuries to a stronghold of the lower middle class from the late Victorian period to the inter-war years. Jews who could afford to escape from the East End moved first to Hackney, but it was the beauty of Stamford Hill that attracted the more ambitious. It clearly exercised a strong appeal which other North-Eastern suburbs did not have. Many Jews had moved to Dalston, Edmonton, Tottenham and Walthamstow but expressed mixed or hostile feelings about these areas: 'Already there are ripenings in Edmonton, Tottenham and Walthamstow, as vile a set of slums as are to be found anywhere'.[3]

But about Stamford Hill we hear more picturesque accounts:

If the traveller looks well about him, he may discern a few old oak and elm trees yet who with their companions long since cut down to clear the ground for building, made this a beautiful hanging wood; and from this summit a splendid view of London as it was then could be obtained.[4]

Walter Besant wrote:

We feel we have got to the end of the world or at any rate to the extreme edges of London – as we stand on the broken heights of green grass and see the sudden drop in the ground which runs away to the stealthily flowing river [the River Lea].[5]

The large houses at reasonable cost attracted the 'upwardly mobile' East End Jews. Tottenham, although nearby, had grown too rapidly as a working-class suburb – in 20 years (1872–92) from 90,000 to 192,000 inhabitants – with 'many miles of small houses to accommodate an immense number of clerks'.[6] Stamford Hill was felt to be a 'cut above', one of the best districts of London's middle-class life.

By the end of the nineteenth century, it had begun its slow decline – smaller houses in terraces were replacing the large villas and their grounds were being built on. Country residences became the only home of their owners who had their businesses in the East End or in the Jewish districts of the West End. During the 1920s and 1930s, Stamford Hill flourished as a solidly lower-middle-class district – a very desirable neighbourhood for respectable Jewish families. Its best-known synagogue was the New[7] – in Egerton Road, right in the heart of Stamford Hill. The United Synagogue had shown foresight in re-establishing the New in Stamford Hill in 1915 and not moving it to the East End, as was strongly argued at the time.

After the Second World War, the Jewish families of Stamford Hill, Stoke Newington and Clapton wanted new homes in the greener reaches of the great north-western outer suburbs. So following the Northern Line of the London Undergound they moved to Hendon, Edgware and Mill Hill and left Stamford Hill in decline. Yet it has survived as a Jewish area, although with a very different kind of Jew. Today, Stamford Hill is a multi-racial area with a mixed urban working-class population. Although the total number of Jews in the district has declined, it has a growing community of Chasidic sects. It is certainly these Jews that now give Stamford Hill its special character.

The settlement of Orthodox Jews is not a new phenomenon in this part of North London. In addition to the strictly Orthodox Finsbury Park Synagogue which had been set up in Lordship Park in the 1880s, the growing numbers of deeply committed Jews of East European background decided to set up a Beth Hamidrash in Canonbury in 1889. By the mid-1890s they wanted to build a *mikveh* (ritual bath) and had moved to Ferntower Road (between Finsbury Park and Stamford Hill). The principal aim of the Beth Hamidrash was 'to encourage the study of the Torah' and they attracted increasing numbers of the Orthodox. In 1905, they moved again, this time to Green Lanes in Stamford Hill, and four years later became the Adath Yisroel (incorporating the North London Beth Hamidrash). This congregation was to become a spearhead of the Orthodox movement; their decision to invite Rabbi Dr Avigdor Schonfield from Hungary to be their leader 'attracted large congregations' to their synagogue.[8] (Their opposition to the Anglo-Jewish establishment was important in the early years of this century as shown by the establishment of the Machzikei Hadath and the creation of the Union of Orthodox Hebrew Congregations.)

Stamford Hill nowadays may have fewer Jews than it had in pre-war times but the vigorous and growing minority of Chasidim, who seem to have taken over some of the main streets, make it obvious that this is still a Jewish district. Clearly Stamford Hill is a centre of the 'black' Adath with their distinctive black trilby hats, long black coats and fur *shtreimel*,* and youths with long *payess*.* All over the area there are Chasidic *shuls*, many following their own Rabbis with total devotion. Special secondary and primary schools exist for the different Chasidic sects: the Lubavitch have their own library and schools in and around the large modern Lubavitch Foundation building near the crossroads of Stamford Hill and Amhurst Park. The Bobov have their own schools, Talmud Torah and *yeshiva** (and their own *shul*) in Egerton Road opposite the New Synagogue – which they recently acquired from the United Synagogue.

Some of the Chasidim prefer the *shtiebl* in the back room of the Rabbi's home; others have lavished considerable sums on large 'complexes' – like the Vishnitz Community which has built a Talmud Torah (school of Hebrew studies) costing over a million pounds. The Vishnitz Synagogue and a Youth Centre are to be incorporated into the new complex. The Satmar are another powerful sect with a centre in Stamford Hill; like the Lubavitch, they followed a Rebbe in New York, Rabbi Yoel Teitelbaum. When he died there in 1976 more than 100,000 people attended the funeral service. The Satmar hold extreme views about Israel which they regard as an improper place for a true Jew. Rabbi Teitelbaum denounced Israel as a 'satanic kingdom'; it had no right to exist before the coming of the true Messiah. Until then for the Satmar and for many other Chasidim it is better to live and pray in Stamford Hill than in Jerusalem.

The area has so many synagogues that it is only possible to list the known ones that are affiliated to the Union of Orthodox Hebrew Congregations:

Ahavat Israel Synagogue d'Chasidey Viznitz

Beth Hamedrash Ohel Naphtoli

Beth Hamedrash Ohel Shmuel Sholem

Beth Hamedrash d'Chasidey Sanz-Klausenberg

Beth Hamedrash Yetiv Lev

Beth Talmud Centre

Kehillath Chasidim Synagogue

Mesifta Synagogue

Beth Hamedrash d'Chasidey Belz

Beth Hamedrash d'Chasidey Gur

Beth Hamedrash Torah Etz Chayim

Beth Hamedrash Torah Chaim

Beth Israel (Trisker) Synagogue

Beth Sholom Synagogue

Birkath Yehuda (Halaser) Beth Hamedrash

Stanislowa Beth Hamedrash

Yeshiva Horomoh Beth Hamedrash

Yeshuath Chaim Synagogue

Yesodey Hatorah Synagogue

Adath Yisroel Tottenham Beth Hamedrash

* See Glossary

The New Synagogue, Stamford Hill, N16

The New Synagogue

It is hard to realise now that this great synagogue was one of the focal points of Jewish religious and communal life in North London. For the Jews of Stamford Hill until the Second World War, the New Synagogue in Egerton Road was as much a landmark as St. Paul's Cathedral. Sadly, the magnificent interior has become shabby and the whole building is a neglected monument to its long history. It is easier to understand the decline of famous synagogues in the East End where the Blitz and the movement of population are obvious causes of the changes. Stamford Hill is, after all, still a Jewish area, even though the type of Jew living there has changed greatly in the post-War period. The many synagogues in Clapton, Stoke Newington and Stamford Hill are mostly small *shtieblach*, set up and frequented by the Chasidim, who thrive and multiply in their own self-imposed ghettos. Large, Anglo-Jewish cathedral-like synagogues do not appeal to them and it is, therefore, curious that the Bobov, a Chasidic community, has taken over the New – the oldest synagogue belonging to the United Synagogue.

The New began as one of the three City of London synagogues serving Ashkenazi Jews in the early years of the eighteenth century. Moses Jacob, a silversmith, left the Great with his friends to set up a synagogue at the Bricklayers' Hall in Leadenhall Street. The breakaway was caused by an increasing number of German Jews in London, dissatisfied with the English ways of the Great Synagogue. The Bricklayers' Hall where Moses Jacob and his fellow rebels set up their New Synagogue was next door to the Cock Tavern. An engraving dated 1811 (see illustration on page 90) entitled, 'The Entrance to a Jews' Synagogue in Leadenhall Street (formerly Bricklayers' Hall)' shows only the doors, next to a tavern and decorated with symbols of the bricklayers' craft. Under the synagogue, wine was stored in a cellar, which inspired a couplet:

> The spirits above are spirits divine;
> The spirits below are spirits of wine.

In the early days of the New, 'spirits' were much less than divine in the very unpleasant quarrels over matters of life and death with the senior synagogue in Duke's Place. The congregation of the New would not associate with the Great on any terms. They established their own burial ground in Brady Street (Stepney). The increasing numbers of poor immigrants led to ugly disputes over problems of relief and burial. In 1790, a pauper's coffin lay in the middle of Duke's Place for a night and a day; neither synagogue would give it burial. The body might have been buried in a nearby church but for a Sephardi Jew who took it to his house and then informed the wardens of Bevis Marks, who persuaded the wardens of the New to bury the body. (In a similar incident four years later, involving a child's burial, the dispute was between the Hambro' and the Great.)

The New remained in Leadenhall Street until 1837 – the year of Queen Victoria's accession to the throne – when its magnificent new building was completed in Great St. Helen's in Bishopsgate. The architect was John Davies and many of the features of his splendid design of the interior can still be seen in the building in Egerton Road. A description of the service of consecration appeared in a weekly journal called the *Mirror*:

> . . . the ceremony of consecrating this edifice sacred to the Jewish religion took place on September 13, 1838; about 1,000 persons being present. The Chief Rabbi and the officiating rabbis having taken their places, the consecration anthem was given. On ordinary occasions the daughters of Zion are kept out of view, in the Asiatic fashion, but on this occasion, although the ladies were all in the galleries, yet the ingenuity of the architect has contrived a handsome screen, so tastefully perforated that the fair sex could see clearly all that was passing below and at the same time those below could easily discover that the Jewish females of our time might vie with those so much admired in ancient times.

The New remained in Bishopsgate in the City throughout Victoria's reign but at the end of the century there were growing demands from the members for it to move to a district nearer the homes of the congregation. The United Synagogue Council decided, in 1912, on Egerton Road in Stamford Hill. (The Great St. Helen's site was sold to M. Samuel and Company and on it now stands Shell Petroleum and its associates in the huge building called St. Helen's Court.)

The existing New Synagogue was designed by Ernest M. Joseph who reproduced the design of the original St. Helen's building as closely as possible. The broad Ark, the *bimah*, the pulpit, the pillars, all vividly recalled the glories of the former synagogue. Much of the interior was brought intact from St. Helen's – even the lamps on the *bimah*, the curtains and silverware as well as the Ark, are the original furnishings. The new 'New' was completed and opened in March 1915.

The 1920s brought a great revival in the fortunes of

* With acknowledgements to M. Bernstein, *Stamford Hill and the Jews before 1915* (London: M.S.B. Publications, 1976).

the New. Stamford Hill had a well-heeled, middle-class Jewish community who filled the synagogue every Sabbath and on the High Holydays, enjoying the splendours of the fine building. It was fully booked for weddings, the interior often lavishly decorated with flowers, the choir gallery filled with boys from the Talmud Torah who could be persuaded to sing.

After reaching its peak in the 1930s, the congregation began to decline at the end of the Second World War. The middle-class Jewish population of Stamford Hill and neighbouring districts moved further out to the new suburbs of Hendon, Southgate, Mill Hill, Edgware and Ilford. The whole area became run-down and depressed: many of the solid, well-kept, late Victorian

Entrance to synagogue in Leadenhall Street (1811)

family houses and Edwardian villas were pulled down and blocks of council flats took their place. The recent revival in the area is largely due to the 'black' Adath – the Chasidic communities who fill the kosher butchers' shops and bakeries in the main streets.

In recent years, the New Synagogue was kept going by a mere handful of elderly members. The only signs of activity were on Sunday mornings when the classrooms of the Talmud Torah and kindergarten were full of the children of the Chasidim. Thus the announcement in the *Jewish Chronicle* (20 February 1987) that the United Synagogue was selling its oldest establishment was not unexpected. The Bobov Community, the new owners, agreed to allow the congregation of the New to use part of the synagogue buildings. The Chasidim intend to use the New mainly for educational purposes.

The 240-year-old New Synagogue has a new lease of life: for how long it is difficult to say.

The North London Progressive Synagogue, Amhurst Park, Stamford Hill

This stronghold of the Liberal and Progressive Movement looks like a Methodist church and, until it was damaged by bombs in the Second World War, the well-preserved building was indeed a nineteenth-century Methodist church. It was restored after 1945 as the Amhurst Park Halls and acquired as a synagogue in 1955 for the congregation which had previously held services in the Library Hall, Stoke Newington, and later at 30 Amhurst Park. The synagogue owes its origins to distinguished Anglo-Jews like Claude G. Montefiore and Lily Montagu, who was its first President.

The first service, conducted by Rabbi Maurice Perizweig, was held in 1921 in the Stoke Newington Library and was attended by over 100 people. There was violent resistance from other Jews to these new forms of Jewish worship and stewards were needed to keep order. The Liberal Progressive form of service and the beliefs of its founders were more radically different from the Orthodox than the ideas and practices of the Reform Synagogues. The difference between a Progressive Synagogue like this one in Amhurst Park and a Reform Synagogue, even a modern suburban one, (apart from a venerable institution like the West London) is quite evident. The stark simplicity of the interior is striking and the main hall was completely

*North London
Progressive Synagogue*

reconstructed in 1961 (architect: Derek Sharpe). The doors of the Ark are made of stainless steel and the *menorah* next to it is made of brass in a modern variation on the traditional theme. Altogether it is an austere, functional design and therefore rather cold.

The immediate past Minister, Rabbi B. Hooker (1975–91) was anything but severe. His tolerance and broad-mindedness even extended to his Chasidic neighbours who help, in his view, to keep the Jewish character of the neighbourhood. Rabbi Hooker associated with other synagogues, whether United or Federation, in the work of combating racism in the area and was represented on the Board of Deputies of British Jews.

The membership of the synagogue is still large (about 1,100) but some no longer live in Stamford Hill nor in the surrounding districts but have moved to the new suburbs in Woodford and Barkingside, where 'daughter' branches of the Amhurst Road Synagogue have been established. Most of the original members have remained in Stamford Hill, but their married children have set up

their homes in the new suburbs. There is an active membership of about 250 people, but the elderly are more likely to attend the Sabbath Morning than the Friday Evening Service as there is some anxiety about risking the journey to *shul* after dark.

The High Holyday Services always attract a capacity congregation of 500–600 people and there is a relatively high attendance for many of the regular services and for the various festivals. One of the attractions is the Cantor who leads the service – unusual for a Progressive synagogue.

Notes

1. A district in Jerusalem.
2. Henry Mayhew, *London Labour and the London Poor*, Vol. II (1851).
3. J. Prag, *Housing Problem* (1901).
4. *Glimpses of Ancient Hackney* (1893).
5. Walter Besant, *East London* (1909).
6. Ibid.
7. From Bishopsgate in the City of London.
8. *The Jewish Chronicle*, 10 December 1909.

6

Three Synagogues in West London

Three synagogues situated in West London, belonging to the three main Orthodox movements, show the social and ethnic divisions within Anglo-Jewry. The Notting Hill, which has now amalgamated with the Shepherd's Bush, Fulham and District, is part of the Federation of Synagogues; the Hammersmith belongs to the United Synagogue; the Holland Park is Sephardi, with close links with Jews from Greece and Turkey. In spite of their differences, each is traditionally Orthodox and maintains the separation of men and women during the service, which is conducted in Hebrew.

Notting Hill Synagogue

The small synagogue in Kensington Park Road has more in common with a traditional *shul* in the East End than with its grand neighbours in Bayswater. This congregation came into being in the late 1890s when the great influx of immigrants from Eastern Europe was at its height. Around Portobello Road a Jewish community settled, largely consisting of tailors, market stall-holders and small shopkeepers. They were poor, industrious, Yiddish-speaking and were used to belonging to a *shtiebl* – or a small *shul*. They were not comfortable in the splendid Bayswater synagogues with upper-class Anglo-Jews. They wanted a small, intimate house of worship where they could *davan* (pray) with their fellow immigrants. Among these immigrants was a Mr Morris Greenberg from Lithuania who conducted the first services of the Notting Hill congregation in 1897 when the *minyan* met at the home of a Mr Cohen in Lancaster Road.

In spite of the differences in wealth and background, it was through the sympathetic help of members of the New West End congregation that the Notting Hill Synagogue was established. Moses Davis, a member of the synagogue in St. Petersburg Place, realised the need

for a smaller synagogue in Notting Hill for the growing community of his fellow Jews in that district. With the approval of Samuel Montagu, Moses Davis acquired a church meeting-hall with two adjoining houses in Kensington Park Road which became the Notting Hill Synagogue and school rooms. It was consecrated in May 1900 and by 1920 it had more than 600 families attending the overflow services required for the High Holydays.

The congregation was at its peak in the 1920s before increasing security and income drew the 'Notting Hillers' to the middle-class houses and green spaces further west in Acton or north-west to Willesden and beyond. In the post-war years the Notting Hill synagogue was one of the first to become affiliated to the Zionist Federation. Chaim Weizmann and Nahum Sokolow spoke from the pulpit and were welcomed by this congregation when Zionism was neither fashionable nor entirely acceptable to Anglo-Jewry. In this Federation Synagogue, Zionist meetings were held or in the shop on the other side of the road known as Sulkin's Corner.

The synagogue was damaged by a bomb during an air raid in the Second World War, but although it has been repaired and reconstructed (in 1952), it is in decline now. There is no Rabbi for the small elderly congregation, but they have a Lay Reader to conduct services. A few years ago the Notting Hill became newsworthy when a bar mitzvah was held for an 83 year-old 'boy'. An American Rabbi from Manhattan, New York, was staying in Kensington with the synagogue's *chazan* (cantor), Stuart Schama. Mr Schama persuaded Rabbi Robuck of Manhattan to conduct the Sabbath service at Notting Hill which included a second bar mitzvah for an elderly widower, Chaim Ozin. According to the *Jewish Chronicle* (9 January 1980) the bar mitzvah was so well received 'that the 70-strong congregation finished

Notting Hill Synagogue

The Hammersmith Synagogue, Brook Green

Ritual silver at Hammersmith Synagogue:
Torah-scroll ornaments, menorah, Kiddush cups

the service by applauding. Relatives from America and from several European countries who had travelled to London for the service had the surprise of their lives when Mr Ozin, after his bar mitzvah, started dancing with the rabbi'.

The interior of the synagogue has recently been renovated and redecorated with the help of an anonymous benefactor. It is a good example of a small traditional synagogue and indeed the central *bimah* and the surrounds of the *Aron Ha-kodesh* (the Ark) are fine examples of traditional craftmanship.

The Hammersmith Synagogue

The oldest of the three, and, indeed, the first to be built in the suburbs of West London is the Hammersmith Synagogue in Brook Green. Until the 1880s the New West End in St. Petersburgh Place, Bayswater, which was established in 1879, was the furthest west. Jewish families, however, had begun to settle further out and were to be found in Hammersmith, Shepherds Bush, Chiswick, Fulham and Barnes, and even as far to the south-west as Kew and Richmond. These suburban settlers found it difficult and inconvenient to attend synagogue in Bayswater, which was hardly within walking distance for most of them. They were concerned too about the lack of religious education for their children in their new districts. In Hammersmith the growing number of Jewish residents presented a clear need for both a local synagogue and religion classes; three men emerged to answer the need and initiated a project to start a synagogue in 1889.

The three founding fathers were Joseph Morris Levy, a shopkeeper in the clothing business, who later became Mayor of Hammersmith; Isaac Morris, a furniture dealer in the Hammersmith Road; and Isaac Sandheim, a dentist. The founders were soon joined by other Jews in Hammersmith, including Delissa Joseph, the architect, who offered his professional services free of charge. A house was found and Joseph prepared plans to adapt it for religious services. At a later date, he also drew up the plans for the permanent building in Brook Green. In spite of some opposition from Delissa Joseph and others, the new Congregation decided to apply to become a Constituent of the United Synagogue at the first meeting of 18 families called to set up the synagogue.

The original building completed in 1890 was unlike the present large and rather grandiose structure, and, according to the *Jewish Chronicle* of that time, 'the smallest Constituent Synagogue of the United Synagogue'. The *bimah* was centrally placed and seemed disproportionately large. In fact it had been planned for the eventual enlargement of the building which was carried out only six years later in 1896. The reconstruction of the synagogue took place in June 1896 and the seating accommodation had been increased to provide for over 400 people – 226 seats for the men on the main floor and 180 for the women in the galleries on three sides of the building. Joseph had followed the continental model by placing the pulpit directly in front of the Ark, thus leaving the maximum room for rows of seats all facing forward to the Ark.

The interior is a curious mixture of an English Methodist meeting hall combined with a nineteenth-century German synagogue on the grand scale. One of the striking features is the pulpit or reading desk to which one ascends by means of carved and curved wooden steps. The Reader's lectern is thus elevated high above and projects over the congregation seated below. Such an arrangement is distinctly hierarchical and no doubt encouraged the Rabbi or Minister to preach to his flock. This may have suited the Reverend Simeon Singer of the highly respectable New West End Synagogue and other United Synagogue Ministers anxious to Anglicise their newly arrived immigrant brethren, but it must have seemed strange to Jews from the ghettos of Eastern Europe who regarded the Rabbi as a teacher but not a preacher. Many of the new immigrants in the last decade of the nineteenth century would have been used to small homely synagogues and may well have been dismayed at the cathedral-like proportions and scale of the enlarged Hammersmith Synagogue.

For much of its 90 years the Synagogue in Brook Green has been the leading establishment in the area and is still very much alive and functioning.

Holland Park

The Spanish and Portuguese Synagogue in Holland Park seems a superior type of establishment compared with its neighbours in Notting Hill and Hammersmith. The restrained brick facade behind the high well-clipped hedge fits in well with the spacious Victorian houses on either side. The only signs that this is a building devoted to non-English activities are the twin cupolas that cap both sides of the roof. St. James's Gardens is a very pleasant square which provides a highly respectable setting for this Sephardi synagogue.

Although the congregation is of mixed ethnic backgrounds, the synagogue grew in response to the needs of Jewish immigrants from the Ottoman Empire just

The Spanish and Portuguese Synagogue, Holland Park

before the outbreak of the 1914–18 War. The Jews who escaped persecution by the Turks came from Salonika in Northern Greece, and from Istanbul. Those who settled in England had other problems to face from the authorities here as they were regarded as enemy aliens and were mostly interned. Before the First World War many of these 'Turkinos' from Salonika settled near the City so that they could worship at Bevis Marks, the synagogue most like their own. The Turkish Sephardim from Istanbul – the Stambolis – settled mainly in West London and gradually a number of families of the Saloniklis also set up homes in Holland Park and Bayswater.

In spite of the traditional differences between the Saloniklis and the Stambolis which might have led at times to their splitting into separate communities, they came together and organised joint meetings in 1924 and a site was purchased in St. James's Square in August of that year. The congregation was originally called 'The Sephardi Congregation of Levantine Jews, London', but in 1926 it was unanimously agreed to change to its present name: The Spanish and Portuguese Congregation, Holland Park.

The interior of the synagogue follows the traditional design with the Ark facing the centrally placed *bimah* which is set well back from the steps leading up to the Ark. Rows of high-backed seats face each other on either side of the *bimah*; the gallery for the ladies is built on three sides of the hall. The interior is well furnished, mainly in dark wood, with white walls and small stained-glass windows on the north and south sides. It is a comfortable and inviting house of worship. A special feature of the service is the reciting of some prayers in Ladino (a Judeo-Spanish dialect) when the Sifrei Torah (the Scrolls) are taken out of the Ark for the second circuit around the congregation.

The Memorial Service held for the victims of the massacre at the Neve Shalom Synagogue in Istanbul in September 1986 took place at the Holland Park Synagogue. The traditions of this London Sephardi Synagogue are close to those of the Neve Shalom and during the simple Memorial Service a confessional prayer recited by Turkish Jews every afternoon was specially added in memory of the victims who died in Istanbul. The Service was arranged by the Board of Deputies which represents all British Jewry, and was attended by many officials of the Christian Churches in England. This sad occasion brought together the leaders of the United Synagogue, the Federation of Synagogues, the Reform Synagogues and the Union of Liberal and Progressive Synagogues.

7

North-West London Synagogues

The Spanish and Portuguese Synagogue, Maida Vale

Although Bevis Marks is the oldest Sephardic synagogue in England, the real centre of Spanish and Portuguese Jewish worship in London is to be found at Lauderdale Road in Maida Vale. This imposing temple of the Sephardim was built in 1895 and is typical of the late Victorian age in its mixture of Gothic, Romanesque and mock-Byzantine features. It is certainly one of the grand designs of the architects Davis and Emmanuel who also built the fine Reform Synagogue in Upper Berkeley Street and the East London Synagogue in Stepney Green.

Whether you sit in the gallery or on the ground floor you feel involved in the Service. The central *bimah* is well designed and the whole interior – the Ark, the seating and the *bimah* are related integrally. Wood is used throughout, including the Ark surround and the panelled doors, which gives warmth and solidity without heaviness. The whole synagogue is well-kept and feels unostentatiously wealthy. It is evidently a place of worship for a congregation which is proud of its synagogue. The interior is very pleasing and the stained-glass windows are particularly beautiful.

The first Spanish and Portuguese Congregation created serious obstacles to the setting up of 'branches' or rival establishments to the original home of the London Sephardim in Bevis Marks. Historically, it is not difficult to understand the insecurity of this small community which re-established the Jews officially in England in the 1650s – the first synagogue to be given public recognition for over 350 years.

Their fervent desire to remain a cohesive community led to the famous Ascama I (Law of the Congregation) enacted in 1664 which forbade 'that there be any other Congregation in this City of London, its districts and environs, for reading prayers with Minyan . . . without separating themselves from the Congregation under pain of Herem [Excommunication] . . .'.

By the nineteenth century, however, this rigid law created serious tensions in the Sephardic Congregation which had now moved to the West End and new suburbs that had developed in St. John's Wood and elsewhere. The ascama and the uncompromising attitudes of the traditional Sephardim led to the most serious and important 'secession' of the century when those who could not change Bevis Marks chose to set up the West London Synagogue of British Jews in 1840 and thus launched the Reform Movement in this country.

Some, of course, remained within the traditional synagogue even though it was inconvenient to walk from their homes in the City. Sir Moses Montefiore, for example, would walk, on the Sabbath, from his fashionable Park Lane residence to the old *snoga* at Bevis Marks where, after Morning Service, he would be entertained for breakfast by the Haham, David Aaron de Sola. The breakfast was usually followed by *Minha* (Afternoon Service) after which he would return to the West End.

Eventually, however, in 1853 the need for a branch synagogue became so marked that a temporary place of worship was opened with the approval of the Mahamad (the ruling body of the Sephardi Congregation) in a house in Wigmore Street. A few years later it became necessary to open a larger and more suitable synagogue in Bryanston Street (near Marble Arch) which served the congregation in the West End for 35 years. The Sephardi population was growing and moving further to the North West, to the new Maida Vale district, and in 1894 a special committee of the Yehidim (the members of the Sephardi Congregation) put forward plans for the erection of a synagogue and a Minister's

The Spanish and Portuguese Synagogue, Lauderdale Road, Maida Vale

house at the junction of Lauderdale and Ashworth Road in Maida Vale. The synagogue was built at a cost of £9,800 and officially opened in 1896. It proved to be an immediate success and led to a resurgence of active membership for the Sephardi community in this part of London. For generations now it has been the main centre for the education of the children of various Sephardi communities, and a Little Synagogue was opened where services are still held fortnightly, conducted by the children themselves.

The New London Synagogue, Abbey Road, NW8

This synagogue owes its special place in Anglo-Jewry to its distinguished Rabbi, Dr Louis Jacobs. The 'Jacobs Affair' was a *cause célèbre* in the mid-1960s and the controversy surrounding Rabbi Jacobs' conflict with the United Synagogue has been exhaustively discussed.[1] What is still relevant is Rabbi Jacobs' influence on Jews who are dissatisfied with the Orthodoxy of the United Synagogue. The New London led by Rabbi Jacobs is independent but, in his words, 'traditional in its service, in its attitude towards the Sabbath and the dietary laws, and in its respect for the values of the past ... Our Synagogue is independent because we have decided to take our destiny into our own hands, to work it out for ourselves ...'. Theologically, Rabbi Jacobs and his followers differ from the mainstream Orthodox in believing that although the Torah was 'divinely inspired', it was not dictated by God, word for word.

The influence of the New London has spread and there are now four other synagogues that follow the teaching of Rabbi Jacobs: the New North London in East Finchley, the Edgware Masorti Synagogue, the New Essex and the South-West London Masorti Synagogue. The name 'Masorti' was chosen because it derives from the Hebrew word *masoret* meaning 'a handing on' in the sense of 'traditional'. In Israel itself, the Masorti is the name adopted by the Conservative movement which is Orthodox but non-fundamentalist. The group of independent Masorti synagogues in London wanted to avoid the name 'conservative' for two reasons: first, they did not wish to appear to be an English equivalent of the American Conservative Synagogues from whom they differ in many ways; second, the word has political associations in England which they wished to avoid.

Rabbi Jacobs is greatly respected in Anglo-Jewry and it is somewhat surprising that more congregations have not followed his synagogue and adopted his approach to Orthodox Judaism. He himself disclaims any ambition to lead a great movement and takes the view that his way can appeal only to an intellectual minority – those Jews who are concerned with the problems of Fundamentalism and those who seek a new approach to being traditional.

The synagogue building was designed by Hyman H. Collins and opened for worship in 1882. It was described at the time as 'Italian with Byzantine feeling' and the red-brick facade is pleasant with graceful columns, but unremarkable as an exterior. The interior has greater charm; in particular, the slender cast-iron columns, the beautiful Ark wall, the unusual pierced grilled balustrade of the Ladies' Gallery and the splendidly designed ceiling all contribute to make a fine example of a late Victorian synagogue. Undoubtedly, the interior was greatly enhanced by the work of Sir Misha Black who undertook the redecoration and restoration of the synagogue when the building was acquired by the congregation in the early 1960s. Fortunately, the building was saved from demolition with only a week's grace. It was sold by the United Synagogue in 1962 for demolition and bought by a property developer, who could not bear to knock it down. He sold it to the New London congregation for the price he had paid for it. (John Betjeman came to see the rescued building and to congratulate the New London Synagogue on saving it.)

The congregation today consists of about 1,100 members, largely affluent middle-class people who live in the expensive north-west residential districts of St. John's Wood, Swiss Cottage and Hampstead. The synagogue offers a full programme of adult educational and cultural activities. An unusual feature is its Youth Group that invites and tries to incorporate all types of synagogue movements in the area.

The St. John's Wood Synagogue

The synagogue in Grove End Road, St. John's Wood, has become the semi-official home of the United Synagogue in London. Its size (one of the largest in Britain), its convenient location (near but not in the West End) and its conference facilities have made it the venue of international meetings for both Jewish and non-Jewish organisations. Not surprisingly, the St. John's Wood Synagogue receives a stream of overseas visitors. The official service in celebration of the centenary of the United Synagogue was held here in 1970. The former Chief Rabbi, Lord Jacobovitz, was a local resident, as is his successor, Dr Jonathan Sacks.

The New London Synagogue, Abbey Road, NW8

The St John's Wood Synagogue, Grove End Road

The ceremonial services to induct them to office were held in this synagogue. The Israeli Ambassador has his official residence nearby and he often attends services in Grove End Road.

The original home of the St. John's Wood congregation in Abbey Road was, in fact, the first synagogue to be founded under the newly created United Synagogue. It was set up in 1876 as a temporary synagogue to meet the needs of the growing Jewish population in the districts of Hampstead, Kilburn and St. John's Wood. The synagogue in Abbey Road was consecrated in 1882 and the first congregation included some outstanding scholars, such as Dr Solomon Schechter[2] and Lucien Wolf.[3] The steady growth of the congregation in the 1880s led to the decision to seek funds from the United Synagogue for a permanent synagogue on the same site in Abbey Road. The new building was designed by H.H. Collins, who designed seven other synagogues, three of which were built for the United Synagogue, and its red-brick Romanesque facade is still a well-known landmark at the corner of Abbey Road and Marlborough Place. This building became the home of the New London Synagogue after the St. John's Wood congregation sold it and moved to larger premises in Grove End Road.[4]

The continuous development of the St. John's Wood Synagogue in size and importance made it necessary to acquire a site on which to build a large permanent structure that would meet the multiple needs of this congregation. The site in Grove End Road was purchased in the mid-1950s and a firm of non-Jewish architects, Bennett and Son, was appointed to design the new building. This same firm was also asked to design another very important United Synagogue building – the Marble Arch – part of the Great Cumberland Place scheme. Thus, a significant and expensive undertaking could not be entrusted to a Jewish architect. The post-war record of the United Synagogue in its decisions affecting three of its most important synagogues in Central London – the Marble Arch, the Central (Great Portland Street) and the St. John's Wood – has hardly been distinguished architecturally. The modern building in Grove End Road seems to have been influenced by the Festival Hall style which combines bulk without elegance. The interior is more striking (see illustration on p.103), at least in the high pointed Ark wall design. The congregation evidently wanted a comfortable, imposing hall of prayer with a high standard of 'finish' and that is what they have. Perhaps it is unrealistic in our time to expect an important synagogue to be as satisfyingly splendid as the great cathedral synagogues

of the past, but exciting new, large, contemporary buildings have been designed in Israel and in the USA by Jewish and non-Jewish architects.

Two Liberal Synagogues

The Liberal Jewish Synagogue in St. John's Wood and the Belsize Square Synagogue in Hampstead both belong to the Union of Liberal and Progressive Synagogues.[4] Apart from this connection, they have little in common in their ritual and their approach to Judaism.

The Liberal Synagogue (the LJS, as it is known) in the wealthy upper-middle class district of St. John's Wood is the oldest and largest Liberal synagogue in England. The founders were Lily Montagu and Claude Montefiore, who had set up the Jewish Religious Union to propagate the ideas of a radical Progressive Judaism. The LJS grew out of the Union and its congregation first held services in 1911. Originally it had met in the West London Synagogue (in Upper Berkeley Street) but broke away when one of the Reform Rabbis refused to let men and women sit together.

The LJS, a famous landmark in North-West London opposite Lord's Cricket Ground – not on the Lord's 'side'! – has recently been demolished. The impressive front of the building with its Grecian columns, the interior with its fine mahogany Ark, the mural by William Uteemohlen depicting the three Festivals of Passover, Pentecost and Tabernacles – all these features which distinguished the 'cathedral' of the Liberal Movement have been replaced by a smaller building with a community centre. Until the new building's consecration and reopening the congregation has been accommodated in a former Anglican Church (All Souls, Loudoun Road, near Swiss Cottage). The LJS, although still a large congregation, has declined from its peak of over 3,000 a few years ago to the current number of 2,100 adult members. Predominantly middle-class and middle-aged, it has widened its range of members and now includes people from many different social backgrounds and a greater variety of occupations: taxi-drivers and market traders as well as doctors, lawyers and businessmen. It is no longer exclusively the upper middle-class, wealthy congregation of the early years and the inter-war period.

The LJS has changed, too, in its Progressive Judaism and in some ways has become more like a Reform synagogue. Significantly, it feels drawn to the West London Synagogue – the cathedral of the Reform Movement. The days of the Jewish Religious Union and the ideas of Lily Montagu and C.G. Montefiore

עברו אח יהוה בשמחה

The Ark of the former Liberal Jewish Synagogue

have gone: the Founders disapproved of bar mitzvah and instituted confirmation in groups for boys and girls at the age of 15 and 16. Nowadays, bar and bat mitzvah (for girls) are held regularly and weekly services are no longer held entirely in English.

There are three Ministers: Rabbi John Rayner, Rabbi David Goldberg and a young woman Rabbi, Alexandra Wright. The senior Minister, John Rayner, feels that the trend towards more traditional practices is inevitable and welcomes the conformity to similar trends in the Reform Movement. Rabbi Rayner is not only in favour of combining in some way with the West London Reform Synagogue but has argued persuasively for a merger of the Reform Movement (the RSGB) with the Liberal and Progressive Movement (the ULPS).

In 1988 (or in the Jewish calendar, 5749) the LJS held its High Holyday Services at the Central Hall, Westminster – a vast building with a huge hall seating 2,600 people. The Central Hall is the focal point of the Methodists' Movement and is as non-denominational a setting as one could find. It is rather an impersonal and non-Jewish place for services celebrating Rosh Hashanah and Yom Kippur but perhaps appropriate for a congregation where many men do not cover their heads and where it is unusual to see a man wearing a *talluth*. Whether at the converted church in Loudoun Road or in the Central Hall, Westminster, this congregation strikes the visitor as much more 'Anglo' than Jewish.

The Belsize Square Synagogue was founded in 1939 by refugees from Germany and Central European states like Austria and Czechoslovakia – the first countries to be 'annexed' by the Nazis. In spite of the fact that Lily Montagu encouraged and helped the new Liberal synagogue to become established and was its first Chairperson, there is not much evidence of her kind of Progressive Judaism in the form of worship at Belsize Square.[5] It owes much more to the nineteenth-century German liberal tradition with its emphasis on music and a Rabbi leading the service entirely in Hebrew. In fact, the Synagogue has a Cantor as well as a Rabbi, a well-conducted choir and the accompaniment of an organ. Men and women sit together as in other Liberal synagogues, but women play a traditional role in that they do not take an active part in the service. To quote from the official prospectus of the synagogue: 'Women may serve as members of our Board and Executive ...' but one can hardly imagine this congregation accepting a woman as their Rabbi.

Originally the congregation occupied a small building in Swiss Cottage, but they now have two spacious buildings in Belsize Square which they acquired in 1947. The membership has grown to more than 1,200 people and seems active and developing. Friday evening (Erev Shabbat) services are unusually well attended. The synagogue provides for different age groups with special services for children held monthly on Sabbath mornings. Rabbi Rodney Mariner, an Australian, leads the congregation with intelligence and wit; the Cantor, Larry Fine, an American, has an exceptionally good voice.

The Hampstead Synagogue

The synagogue in Dennington Park Road, West Hampstead, is a Constituent of the United Synagogue, but its congregation has a history of non-conformity and of innovation which sets it apart from the typical Orthodox community. Hampstead itself is a district that has attracted Jewish and non-Jewish intellectuals and artists – those successful enough to afford to live there – and professional people (architects and psychiatrists are well represented in the area) since the 1880s when Hampstead Village began to grow and become submerged into the London suburbs. By the 1890s there were a considerable number of Jewish families in West Hampstead and Kilburn, and only one synagogue in St. John's Wood to cater for local needs. Some of the Hampstead intellectuals who were concerned with Judaism formed a circle called 'The Wanderers', which included Herbert Bentwich and Israel Zangwill, a group dominated by the personality of Solomon Schechter. Norman Bentwich (the son of Herbert) described them thus: 'The Wanderers were a kind of Fourth Party in Anglo-Jewry, concerned to make Judaism a living force and in arms against the complacent respectability of both lay and spiritual leaders'.

In May 1889, Herbert Bentwich wrote a letter to the *Jewish Chronicle* inviting support for the idea of a Synagogue in Hampstead and a committee was formed to ... 'ascertain the desirability of establishing forthwith a Synagogue in the Hampstead district'. The original committee included some of the 'Wanderers' and members of all three congregational bodies of Anglo-Jewry of that time: the United Synagogue, the Sephardi Synagogue and the West London Reform Synagogue. Their ambitious aim was to launch a movement which would combine elements of both Orthodoxy and Reform. Among their specific innovations were:

> that a small part of the Service be read in English;
> that repetitions of prayers, including the Sabbath 'Amidoth' be omitted;

The Hampstead Synagogue, Dennington Park Road

that the *duchan** ceremony be abolished;

that a Service for the Confirmation of girls be
introduced.

In fact, a motion in favour of association with the
Reform Movement was proposed in the committee but
was defeated. It was decided that the Congregation
accept the authority of the Chief Rabbi, but Dr Nathan
Adler, who was in office at that time, was not prepared
to accept some of the basic points in the committee's
programme. Several members of the committee resigned, but after the death of Dr Nathan Adler in 1892
discussions were again held with the new Chief Rabbi,
Dr Hermann Adler (son of the former Chief Rabbi). At
a special conference on ritual matters some modifica-
tions were agreed.

The special character of the Hampstead Synagogue
was thus present at its origins: a Congregation whose
leaders were prepared for controversy in the cause of
changes to modernise the traditional Service, but always
wanting to stay within the Orthodox Movement and
remain a United Synagogue.

The Hampstead Synagogue, consecrated in 1892,
was designed by Delissa Joseph, who was also the
architect of the Hammersmith and West Kensington
Synagogue. An unusual feature in Hampstead is the
octagonal shape of the building, and it was the first
Synagogue in England to follow the European tradition
of placing the *bimah* and pulpit on a platform in front
of the Ark. In 1897, in honour of Queen Victoria's
Diamond Jubilee, classrooms, a Board Room and a
Sukkah were erected at the side of the building. Several
sets of stained-glass windows have been installed,
mostly in memory of past members of the congregation.
The first window of the series on the ground floor
depicting the Twelve Tribes of Israel was presented by
the Reverend Green and his wife in memory of their
son. The Rev. Green became the first Minister of the
Hampstead Synagogue in 1892 and remained with the
congregation for 40 years.

Edward Jamilly sums up the notable features of
Hampstead Synagogue:

... with a tower, not common to Synagogues, and
Romanesque detail in dark red brick. The unique
octagonal domed interior comes nearer perhaps *than
any Synagogue so far to the spirit of its time*, that
interlude between the Arts and Crafts and Pre-
Raphelite Movements and the plunge into Art
Nouveau. Hampstead was notable also for the combination of Ark, Reader's platform and pulpit at one

* See Glossary

end of the building, greeted as the first adoption in
London of the 'Continental' (i.e. 'liberal') arrangement. This, too, was enlarged but lost the original
wooded Ark with its fine, sweeping steps for a
misconceived improvement ...[6]

Hampstead Synagogue is justly proud of its long and
rich musical tradition. At its foundation ceremony it
was involved in dispute with the Chief Rabbi who
objected to the 'mixed' (men and women) choir's
participation at the ceremony. Apart from this particular
ceremony, the synagogue persisted until recently in
retaining a mixed choir, which sang regularly from
the Sabbath onwards. Samuel Alman joined the congregation in 1916 and his musical partnership with the
Cantor, the Reverend Gershon Boyars (Chazan in the
1930s), led to his choral compositions being sung in
synagogues throughout the world.

The traditional Orthodox synagogue has been slow
to allow Jewish women to participate fully and publicly.
The Hampstead Synagogue, unlike other United Syna-
gogues, led the way in introducing Confirmation for
girls. Three years before the synagogue was opened, the
Hampstead committee had recommended (in 1889) 'that
a Service for the Confirmation of girls . . . be instituted
in the proposed Synagogue following the model of the
Service adopted at the Central Synagogue'. And the
Chief Rabbi, Dr. N.M. Adler, had agreed to the proposal!
In fact, the first special service for girls was held by the
Reverend Green in July 1895. Now, there are annual
Bat Chayil ceremonies in all United Synagogues.

Since the end of the last century the Hampstead
Synagogue has played a significant part in the development of Anglo-Jewry's Orthodox Movement. To quote
Rabbi Raymond Apple, Minister of the Synagogue
from 1965 until 1972:

Hampstead has always been more than simply a local
house of worship for Jewish residents in a particular
district of London . . . The men who founded Hampstead were men of unusual personality and ideals and
living in an age of religious restlessness they set out
not only to erect a building but to initiate a religious
movement.[7]

Yet it must be said that there are those who have
always felt that the aims of the Founders have not been
achieved, nor is Hampstead Synagogue in any real sense
a radical version of an Orthodox congregation. Rabbi
Apple has also described how . . . 'even Bentwich eventually left the Synagogue in disillusionment, feeling as
others have done, both then and in later years, that far
from becoming a dynamic movement, Hampstead had

The octagonal domed interior at Hampstead Synagogue

developed into a citadel of prosperous respectability'.[8]

No-one would deny that the synagogue in West Hampstead is impressive in the dignity of its services, the quality of its sermons and the high standard of its cantorial and choral music. Dignity and decorum are good qualities, but it has been suggested that the atmosphere of Hampstead has often seemed cold and patronising to outsiders. This is certainly not a 'heimish' congregation, nor is such a fine building conducive to the warmth and intimacy of a *shtiebl*, but it has certainly changed since the days when silk hats and frock coats were *de rigueur* on a Sabbath. Hampstead Synagogue today maintains its fine traditions and is very much a living institution which still inspires much devotion and great loyalty in its members.

Two Synagogues in Hampstead

Two small synagogues exist within a few yards of each other yet are miles apart in their forms of worship and their concepts of Judaism. The Hampstead Adath and the Hampstead Reform lie at opposite ends of the Jewish spectrum. In the Reform Congregation men and women sit together and the women play as large a part in the reading or leading the service as the men. In recent years, the Hampstead Reform even had a woman Rabbi. The Adath Synagogue strictly divides the male worshippers from the female, who are hidden behind a curtained partition during the service.

The Hampstead Adath Yisroel Congregation was founded as the Sarah Klausner Memorial Synagogue (in memory of the mother of Arnold Klausner, a businessman, who donated the money for the building in Broadhurst Gardens, West Hampstead). The original congregation had been established in Bow in East London but the synagogue was destroyed by bombing in 1940. It was re-established in Compayne Gardens (West Hampstead) after the war in 1947. It has the feeling and atmosphere of a *shtiebl* but not quite of the traditional kind. The members of the congregation are not poor tailors or small shopkeepers but middle-class professional and business men. Although there is no membership charge, the congregation are expected to donate to the funds to cover overheads.

The moving spirit behind the revival of the tiny synagogue in recent years is Mr Leslie Levens, a local resident, who has personally financed the renovation of the building and paid for its furniture and fittings. Mr Levens is as proud of their special *kiddush* after Sabbath Services as the chef of a famous restaurant. There is no doubt that it is attractive to the members as Mr Levens

provides 'a supreme mixture of delicacies, inclusive of smoked salmon, pickled herring, onions, crisps, cakes, biscuits and, of course, plenty of wine and whisky'. The basic appeal of this old-fashioned *shul* is, of course, its very old-fashionedness and its adherence to Orthodoxy. In its own eyes, it is 'maintaining the high Jewish standards associated with the Adath Yisroel'. Unlike the Chasidim with their Yiddish culture and their guru-like Rabbis, the Adath Synagogue is a refuge from the modern world which allows the adherent to be an Anglo-Jew in his ordinary daily life. There is a kind of nostalgic return to the past in this growth of the *shtiebl* which seems to be spreading in similar small congregations in other parts of North-West London.

The Hampstead Reform Community started about ten years ago without a synagogue building. A few like-minded Reform Jews with strong religious convictions began meeting regularly for Friday Evening Services in one another's homes. The congregation grew partly through the devoted work of a few families and a number of individuals who loyally supported their meetings. The small community acquired the services of a part-time Rabbi and a few years ago took the big step of leasing a small building (formerly a shop with an upper floor which could be used for services) in West Hampstead. They continue to hire the Quakers' Meeting Hall in Hampstead, for the High Holydays. Their second Rabbi was Barbara Borts, a young American, and their present part-time Minister is Samuel Pereira, a Reform Rabbi with a Sephardic background.

The Hampstead Reform Community can no longer afford its own premises and now meets in a large room in Hashomer House which is run by the Israeli Mapam Organisation. In spite of its lack of funds and without its own synagogue, this small congregation survives against all the odds. It does not seem to have a strongly religious appeal for most of its members, although this is the common denominator binding it together. It is really a Reform *chevra* with social activities (food fairs, rambles, etc.) and friendly people for the lonely. It continues its Friday Evening Services in private homes (mostly at the home of the Chairperson who is the Mother and Shepherd of her flock) and obviously provides a religious-social club which fills a need for people living in impersonal London districts like West Hampstead. The services themselves are read as much in English as possible with only the most sacred prayers like the 'Shema Yisroel' and the *kaddish* chanted or sung in Hebrew.

The congregation has always welcomed converts,

Dollis Hill Synagogue

and no-one who has difficulty in reading Hebrew needs to feel left out. The Rabbi is a curious mixture of old and new teacher and preacher. Deeply learned in Jewish and sacred history, he seems to be strangely 'un-Reformed' and clings to his Sephardic background, but the more his congregation get to know his mind the more they respect his deep convictions and understand that his tolerance could only find a home in the Reform or Liberal synagogue.

Both these small *shtiebl*-like synagogues, for all their differences, have something in common which is important to their congregations. Their very smallness is part of their appeal, especially in a vast city like London. Jews, like other people, want to feel they belong to communities where they are noticed and

recognised. The large synagogue, whether United or Reform, does not always provide for these deep human needs.

Dollis Hill Synagogue
Parkside, Dollis Hill Lane, NW2

Designed by Sir Owen Williams, this remarkable modern synagogue building set in an unfashionable north-western suburb, boldly gives a new form to the structure of the synagogue that is not a compromise between a church and a Moorish temple nor yet another 'functional' post-war box. It has been described as 'one of the most noteworthy of twentieth-century Jewish religious buildings'[9] and 'almost the only one that told the world Judaism was a modern religion and alive in England'.[10]

The United Synagogue was not happy with the design, and the new building is still spoken about by the parent body as an experience they would not like to repeat. Nevertheless, students of architecture and visitors from many other countries have shown great interest and admiration for the unusual synagogue.

The Dollis Hill Synagogue was built in 1937 and consecrated early in 1938. Sir Owen Williams, an outstanding Welsh engineer, had it constructed entirely in reinforced concrete without columns. From the front it has a low bulky vestibule and a higher level containing the main hall with accordion-pleated walls. On three sides it has hexagonal and arched windows and the whole exterior is painted a stark white. From the outside it is strikingly successful; the interior is much more conventional with the pulpit and Reader's desk on a raised platform in front of the Ark, leaving the rest of the ground floor for rows of seats for the male members of the congregation. The cantilevered galleries for the ladies are more unusual in structure, and the six-sided windows with symbolic coloured images (signs of the Zodiac, symbols of the main Festivals and the Twelve Tribes of Israel) surrounding the hall help to brighten the interior. The synagogue is quite large, with seats for more than 900 people.

Shortly after the end of the Second World War, the synagogue suffered an act of vandalism reminiscent of Nazi Germany, which was a considerable shock in post-war Britain. During the night of 29 December 1946, the synagogue was broken into and all twelve of the sacred Sifrei Torah (the Scrolls) were destroyed, together with a number of Bibles and prayer books. The vandals also destroyed the Reader's desk and started a fire in front of the Ark, which was seriously damaged. The Congregation's dignified response to the attack was a solemn Service of Remembrance held a few weeks later. The remains of the destroyed Sepharim (the holy books) were buried at the Willesden U.S. Cemetery in the grave of the scribe, Moses Halperin.

Today the synagogue is rather too large for the congregation, which has declined to about 300 members. (On the Sabbath between 40 and 50 members attend the service.) The district no longer attracts young Jewish families, so the congregation (like so many in Central London), is becoming elderly. The presiding Minister, the Reverend Taylor, has been with the synagogue since 1951 but is no longer full-time. He is now the *Chazan* (Cantor), and weekly Sabbath Services are conducted by Rabbi B. Susser. The Rabbi and the Wardens welcome visitors and are more than willing to show their outstanding example of modern synagogue architecture.

Notes

1. See the section in Ch. 4 on the New West End Synagogue.
2. Dr Solomon Schechter (1850–1915), scholar and theologian.
3. Lucien Wolf (1857–1930), journalist and historian.
4. For the restoration of the Abbey Road Synagogue in 1965 by Sir Misha Black see p.101 above.
5. The Belsize Square Synagogue has recently become independent and is therefore no longer affiliated to the ULPS.
6. Edward Jamilly, 'Synagogue Art and Architecture' in Salmond S. Levin (ed.), *A Century of Anglo-Jewish Life* (London: United Synogogue, 1971).
7. Raymond Apple, *The Hampstead Synagogue, 1892–1967* (London: Vallentine, Mitchell, 1967).
8. Ibid.
9. Carol Krinsky, *The Synagogues of Europe* (Cambridge, MA: The M.I.T. Press, 1985).
10. Jamilly, 'Synagogue Art and Architecture'.

8

Golders Green and its Synagogues

Golders Green has become synonymous with 'Jewishness' and is almost as central to London Jewish life as the East End was before the Second World War. Kosher restaurants (Bloom's in Golders Green Road is busier than the original Bloom's in Whitechapel), kosher butchers and poulterers, an Israeli Bank, Jewish bookshops and bakeries are all to be found in the main street of this bustling district. On Chanukah, the Chasidim of the area erect a huge *menorah* in the courtyard of Golders Green Underground Station. Every evening for eight nights a London 'celebrity' is invited to light the candles, which is quite a performance as they have to be lifted by crane to the right height.

Every type of synagogue can be found in NW11 from the Reform to the most Orthodox. In addition to the known and established synagogues, there are *shtieblach* where the Orthodox followers of a particular Rabbi or rabbinic family worship and meet for Talmudic study. The services usually take place in the Rabbi's house as these congregations are small.

Without attempting a comprehensive survey of the synagogues of Golders Green, the following selection gives an idea of the leading ones representing a cross-section of the Synagogue Movements.

The Golders Green Synagogue

The large imposing building in purple-red brick in Dunstan Road houses the oldest synagogue in Golders Green. Even more impressive inside, this is a splendid survivor of the pre-war Anglo-Jewish synagogue. One can believe that it was described as the 'flagship' of the United Synagogue when it was consecrated in 1922. (The foundations of the buildings were laid by Lionel de Rothschild, MP in 1921.) On the Sabbath, with the top-hatted *shammas** and the high-backed throne-like

* See Glossary

seats for the Rabbi and the Cantor, the atmosphere is very formal. The dignity of the ritual and the surroundings are reminiscent of the great Jewish 'cathedrals' of a century ago.

The interior is spacious and ornate; the central *bimah* is solid wood surrounded by brass railings in the shape of *menorahs*. The Ark has three carved mahogany columns; the marble pulpit is approached by means of curved steps and brass rails. The Ladies' Gallery is supported by twelve white columns which extend above the galleries to the high ceiling; stained glass windows surround the building (except, of course, on the eastern side above the Ark), ten at ground-floor level and ten more around the Ladies' Gallery. The building was designed by Digby L. Solomon entirely on traditional lines, and it fits in well with its eminently respectable surburban surroundings.

Traditional Orthodox synagogues in the moderate United Synagogue pattern are having a difficult time in many areas. Golders Green has, of course, many small synagogues for the more extreme Orthodox Jews in the district. Dunstan Road is very aware of the attractions of the Adath congregations with their warmth, their religious fervour and their welcoming intimacy. The Golders Green Synagogue is very dignified but it can seem pompous and remote to the younger Jew.

Some of the younger active members of this congregation are worried about the top-hats and the formal image of their long-established synagogue. They want to attract other young people and there are encouraging signs that their campaign to halt the decline in membership has succeeded. The synagogue has about 800 members and this number is being maintained. The Rabbi, Ivan Binstock, is actively promoting an increase in the educational facilities and they offer three Shabbat youth services – for under-eights, for eight to twelve-year-olds and for the post-bar mitzvah students. New

The Golders Green Synagogue

members are being recruited in a variety of ways by appealing to London University students and by opening a new nursery school. Altogether there is much activity and an atmosphere of enthusiasm and revival at Golders Green's oldest synagogue.

Beth Abraham Synagogue

No. 46, The Ridgeway, looks just like any other semi-detached house in this street of two-storeyed family houses with a small front garden and a larger back garden. Inside it is a small synagogue – a *shtiebl* – and on the Sabbath it hums with activity. The typical *chevra* of the East End must have been very like this except for the air of relative prosperity. The congregation of this Adath Congregation is neither poor nor working-class; nor is it particularly well-off.

The ground floor of the house has been enlarged with an extension into the garden and it has been partitioned to separate the men from the women. The men's part of the room is usually very crowded with about 50 men and boys having just enough room to stand or sit at long wooden tables on which they lean and study the *siddurim* (prayer books). The women pray behind a glass screen covered with lace curtains which enables them to see a little of the service but not be seen. Fewer women and girls attend the services than men, for this is where the Jewish male predominates even more obviously than in the Orthodox United Synagogue service.

The congregation seems to be constantly moving even when the members are silently praying. They sway, bow and move rhythmically as they read, repeat or chant the prayers. Except when an important prayer is being spoken by the whole congregation, some members are entering or leaving the Service, adding to the sense of perpetual motion: it is very devout and devoted but not an ideal atmosphere for silent contemplation.

The room is simply furnished with a couple of Reader's desks in front of the Ark, which itself is only a tall cupboard covered with the usual blue velvet cloth embroidered with Hebrew lettering in gold thread. A simple hanging electric lamp acts as the *ner tamid* (eternal light) suspended in front of the Ark. The Rabbi does not often play an active role in the service but moves around the congregation quietly, admonishing the restless boys or congratulating those who have read their portion of the Torah aloud to the rest of the congregation. The older men mostly wear a woollen *talluth* with which they cover their heads when praying. Nearly all the young men wear dark blue wide-brimmed trilby hats and formal dark lounge suits. Yiddish is the language of everyday communication as much as English, especially among the middle-aged and elderly men.

Strangers are made to feel very welcome, provided they look as if they have come to pray and to participate seriously. You will immediately be handed a book all in Hebrew or a 'Singer's' which is the traditional prayer book of the Orthodox with its English translations of the Hebrew Service. You will be closely questioned in a friendly manner: 'Where are you from? Where are you staying in the district? Have you somewhere to go and eat after the service? If not, come with us.' You will be included and looked after. The people of this congregation are direct and have no pretensions – sure of themselves and of their place in the community. The strongest impression is of a family who meet regularly and unquestioningly for a common purpose. The Rabbi is the father, and all the congregation, young, not-so-young and old, are the children. You feel the warmth and the bonds even if your mind tells you it depends on absolute acceptance of the ritual and the authority of the Rabbi.

The North Western Reform Synagogue

The synagogue in Alyth Gardens, Finchley Road, NW11, is widely known as a centre for Reform Jews and has a large congregation. In addition to its synagogue, 'Alyth' has an active social life for its own community and for the disabled through its close connection with the Barnet voluntary services.

Originally founded in 1933, it held its first services in a private home in Golders Green; the first High Holyday services were held in the Hampstead Garden Suburb Centre. These days the congregation is large enough to fill the Odeon Cinema in Finchley where indeed High Festival services have been held. Many German Jewish refugees settled in the area and were drawn to this Reform synagogue. The architect of the synagogue's Sanctuary and the artist who designed the bronze plaque of the Ten Commandments over the entrance were both refugees from Germany. The present synagogue building was opened in 1935: its stained-glass windows were designed and made by Roman Halter on the theme of 'The Celebration of Life' depicting in its 18 window scenes of Israel, images of nature and inscriptions from the Bible. On the walls there are some fine tapestries made by members of the congregation to celebrate 'Alyth's' fiftieth anniversary.

The Golders Green Beth Hamedrash Congregation

Universally known as 'Munk's Shul', the Golders Green Beth Hamedrash congregation was formed in 1933 by a small group of Orthodox Jews who held Sabbath Morning services in the library of King Alfred's School. Rabbi Munk became their first Rabbi in 1934 and remained with the Congregation until he retired in 1968. In 1935 larger premises became necessary and in that year the Lincoln Institute in Broadwalk Lane was consecrated, comprising a synagogue, a library and class-rooms for the adult study circles which have always been an important part of the community's activities. The congregation continued to grow and in 1955 the new synagogue in the Riding, Golders Green Road, NW11, was begun and completed in 1959. (The Chief Rabbi, Dr Israel Brodie, officiated at the ceremony of consecration on 20 September 1959.) Rabbi Haim Feldman succeeded Rabbi Munk in 1968 and continues to be the Minister.

The Sinai Synagogue, 54 Woodstock Avenue, NW11, established in 1935, is a constituent of the Federation of Synagogues. Its Minister is Rabbi M.L. Flax.

The following *shtiebl*-type *shuls* are all constituent members of the Union of Orthodox Hebrew Congregations:

Beth Abraham Synagogue, 46 The Ridgeway, NW11

Beth Hamedrash, 137 Golders Green Road, NW11

Beth Hamedrash d'Chasidey Gur, 16 The Drive, NW11

Beth Hamedrash Divrei Chaim, 71 Bridge Lane, NW11

Beth Shmuel Synagogue, 171 Golders Green Road, NW11

9

Synagogue Architecture in London

A survey of the architecture of London synagogues and the decorative art within the buildings leaves us with unanswered questions. Why, with so many synagogues, are there so few that are bold or beautiful? And why do many lack distinctively Jewish features? (It is small comfort that a similar survey of church building in London in the last 100 years would have little to show that was better.) The questions remain, and to understand the problems it is worth examining the complex relationship between the synagogue authorities and architects, the congregations and the social context within which they have had to live and interact.

Over the past three centuries, since the Resettlement, British Jews have slowly emerged as full citizens; until very recently they have felt insecure about showing their Jewish identities in this country. It was not always safe to be seen or heard in England even in the period of 'Toleration and Emancipation'. Synagogues were built but hidden away in courtyards or merged discreetly into the street. Not until the Victorian age did synagogue buildings assert themselves and really go public. The great Anglo-Jewish cathedrals of the late nineteenth century were not distinctively Jewish, at least not in external appearance. The London synagogues of that period are Victorian buildings with all the characteristic features: rose windows, Romanesque arches, towers, domes and colonnaded entrances, splendid interiors – such as the New West End in Bayswater – and a mixture of styles that can only be described as 'mishu-Gothic'!

The major influence dominating London synagogue architecture over the last 120 years has been the United Synagogue. The governing bodies of this Orthodox movement were responsible for the design and building of more than 80 synagogues from 1870 to 1970. They deliberately imposed a policy of Anglicisation. The hierarchy of the United Synagogue used its great financial power over the planning and design of syna-

gogues to mould the congregation into a particular model. It has not gone unchallenged but it was the major force. From 1880 to 1914, the settled Anglo-Jewish community was profoundly shaken and changed by the massive immigration from Eastern Europe and Russia. The struggle that ensued was social, political and religious and in this conflict between the West End Establishment and the 'alien' ways of the East End, architects and synagogue designs were weapons to be used by those who paid for the buildings.

From 1870, through its central funds, the United Synagogue provided about one-third of the cost of the site and the building of a synagogue. Those synagogue buildings that failed to meet certain requirements were rejected. The United Synagogue laid down designs and features that were deemed 'acceptable'; the traditional type of arrangement of the service was explicitly regarded as alien, leading to unruly ways and unfavourably contrasted with the pious behaviour in church services. Clearly, some Jewish religious practices – members of the congregation praying at their own pace – favoured too much congregational participation and thus, too little direction by the Reader. The older tradition of the synagogue as a meeting-place (*beth haknesset*) was to be replaced by a building solely designed for worship. The 'U.S.' design which became dominant aimed at imposing a standardised service with orderly prayers led by a Minister in a standardised format.

What was the United Synagogue lay-out and who were the architects chosen to implement the planning? Significantly, the internal arrangement (illustrated on p.119) moved the central reading desk (*bimah*) – its traditional position – to a platform in front of the Ark, next to the pulpit. To emphasise the role of the Rabbi/ Minister as preacher, the pulpit became more prominent in front of the Ark. The most extreme example of

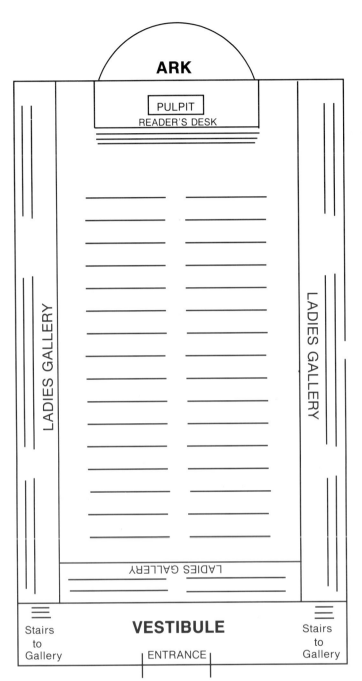

*Ground plan of the United Synagogue standard interior –
allowing provision of maximum seating for men, ladies' gallery
on three sides (north, west and south) and combined pulpit/reader's
desk in front of the Ark.*

the 'Anglicised' arrangement can be seen in the large
Hammersmith Synagogue (1896) where the pulpit is
high above and projects over the seated congregation
(see p.96).

The late Victorian synagogues show a multi-
plicity of styles often in conflict: Gothic shapes and
Romanesque arches proclaim Anglicised Westernness;
the Mooresque domes and cupolas, Spanish-style

screens and oriental details provide the Jewish trap-
pings. The overall effect was of a Jewish house of
worship acceptable to English taste.

The architects were a small élite chosen by the
'Grand Dukes' of the United Synagogue. Nathan S.
Joseph, Chairman of the Board of Guardians, the
brother-in-law of the Chief Rabbi, was the Architect-
Surveyor of the United Synagogue. He designed some
of the principal 'cathedrals' of the late Victorian period:
the Central (1870), the Bayswater (partly his design)
(1863); the New West End (1878) and the Dalston
(1885). His nephew, Delissa Joseph, was responsible
for the beautiful Hampstead Synagogue (1892),
the Hammersmith (1890) and Hackney (1897).
Unlike previous generations of synagogue designers
who had been non-Jews, the 'U.S.' did employ Jewish
architects and in addition to the Joseph family, there
were Hyman Collins (eight synagogues including Abbey
Road, St. John's Wood and the North London, Barns-
bury (1868)), Davis and Emanuel who designed the East
London (1876) and the West London Reform in Upper
Berkeley Street, and Edward Salomons (who designed
the Manchester Synagogue), the principal architect of
the Bayswater (1863).

The dominant model carefully planned by the United
Synagogue and its architects was, however, being
threatened by the mushroom growth of *chevrot* and the
religious fervour in the East End. Before 1870, Jewish
immigrants (mainly from the Netherlands and Germany) had set up *chevrot* by converting Nonconformist
chapels into small synagogues (e.g Sandy's Row). The
newer waves of East European immigrants after 1880
set up *chevrot* and *shtieblach* in such profusion as to alarm
the West End Establishment. Like their tailors' workshops, they were independent and self-supporting and
their *chevrot* were not going to fit into the United Synagogue's Anglicised ways. These small *shuls* did not
recognise the authority of the Chief Rabbi nor did they
have much respect for Anglo-Jewry. Orthodox Jews
from Eastern Europe were more in sympathy with
Rabbis of the Machzikei Hadath (Spitalfields Great)
which directly opposed the United Synagogue and its
Anglicised Orthodoxy. The challenge from 'the Torah
fortress in Anglo-Jewry',[1] however, became much less
threatening when in 1905 it accepted loans from the
United Synagogue to pay for building debts. In return
for this help, the Machzikei Hadath agreed to recognise
the authority of the Chief Rabbi. The small East End
congregations were condemned by the West End
establishment as unsafe and insanitary. Settled Anglo-
Jewry was genuinely worried by the alarming growth of

the *chevrot* in which subversive radical movements and Zionists were becoming active. We have to bear in mind that the Anglo-Jew had only recently gained his relatively secure position in English society. All the hard-won security and respectability seemed threatened by these Eastern European Yiddish-speaking immigrants setting up their separate societies and their makeshift *shtieblach* in East London.

The United Synagogue, as the leading Anglo-Jewish body, did more than merely condemn the growth of the *chevrot* and small synagogue. It initiated positive measures to bring order and control to the 'anarchy' in the East End. First, the United Synagogue encouraged the building and conversion of synagogues in districts beyond Whitechapel and Stepney. As a result, synagogues were built in North-East and North London in Hackney, Stoke Newington and on the fringe of East London in Stepney Green. In the latter part of the 1870s, three major synagogue buildings exemplified the United Synagogue policy: the East London, the Stoke Newington and the Hackney. All three had to conform strictly to the United Synagogue norm: economical construction (largely using brick) and 'the plainest character'.[2] The central committee of the 'U.S.' ensured that the exteriors were similar and made to merge with the housing in the street, most notably in the case of the East End Synagogue, which is plain to the point of drab ugliness on the outside, yet has a splendidly Byzantine design inside the building. The pulpit in all three is placed in front of the Ark and is clearly meant to become the focal point; no longer would the congregation have its central *bimah* and the Ark as the centres of attention. As we have seen,[3] Joseph Stern, the outstanding Minister of the East London, consciously used his pulpit to preach the doctrine of Anglicisation to the Jews of Stepney Green.

Second, some of the leading members of Anglo-Jewry adopted an enlightened policy of assisting the *chevrot* to become properly established small synagogues. The West End decided to control and Anglicise the East End by encouraging the *chevrot* to form their own association. The Federation of (Minor) Synagogues consisted originally of 21 existing congregations. In 1903, Sir Samuel Montagu gave evidence to the Royal Commission on Alien Immigration and described the conditions in the 'isolated minor synagogues in the East End of London' and his aims: 'to get rid of the insanitary places of worship and to amalgamate two or three small ones and have a suitable building . . .. At present we have thirty-nine synagogues in the Federation . . . chiefly in Whitechapel and Stepney.

We cater for the working classes among Jews'.

The leaders of the Federation, although close to the needs and feelings of working-class Jews, adopted United Synagogue politics and standards. In 1896, the concept of a 'model synagogue' appeared which clearly aimed to change the prevailing *chevra/shtiebl* into a West End type of synagogue, albeit on a smaller scale to suit the East London street. During the 1890s, the policy of Montagu and the Federation made a marked difference to the life of the East London congregation. Typically, two *chevrot* which had met in private houses in Philpot Street or Fieldgate Street, joined together and found themselves eligible for funds which could be arranged with the help of Montagu. A new 'model' synagogue would come into being: many were designed by Lewis Solomon, the chief architect of the Federation. Few of these small synagogues still exist but the new model, approved by the West End, soon came to dominate the East End congregation. The Federation type of synagogue can still be seen in Fieldgate Street and in Princelet Street; the most typical of the new 'amalgamated' synagogues built in the 1890s were the New Road, Whitechapel and the Old Castle Street synagogues; both of these were destroyed by bombs in the Second World War.

The United Synagogue and its less powerful 'sister' group, the Federation, continued to be the dominant influence on buildings and their congregations right through the first half of this century. Increasingly, however, social change and the movement of London's Jewish population have challenged and undermined middle-of-the-road Orthodoxy. The old struggle between East End and West End became irrelevant. During and after the Second World War, the Jews left Whitechapel and Stepney and moved to the new suburbs.

Since 1945, the largest new synagogues have been built in Edgware (1956), Finchley (1966) and in Ilford – all United Synagogue congregations and none of them in Central London. The position of the West End synagogue is problematical, even the so-called 'magnificent seven'[4] have an uncertain future. The buildings were constructed on a large scale to accommodate fashionable congregations who lived in Central London. Wealthy Jews and their families are now more likely to live in Finchley or Hampstead Garden Suburb – and belong to a local synagogue – than to reside in Mayfair or Bayswater. Although it was constructed in the same year (1937) as the striking Dollis Hill Synagogue, the Hampstead Garden Suburb Synagogue, Norrice Lea, is much more typical of 'U.S.' architectural style in the post-war period. The Norrice Lea building has a bland exterior and a 'period'-type interior (Dutch-style candelabra, expensive wood panelling). It is all done in the best taste and is carefully neutral. A more ambitious large building is the Edgware Synagogue, erected in 1956. Although an expensive project, it is said that the architect was forced to save money by designing the building to include steel roof trusses salvaged from a Festival of Britain exhibit. The resulting community building looks like a mixture of aircraft hangar and municipal gymnasium. Fortunately, perhaps, the Edgware Synagogue was built beside a motorway and its bulk is not too prominent.

It is sad that not one distinguished British, European or even American architect in the post-war period has been commissioned to design a synagogue in the Greater London area. So many new communities and congregations have settled in the outer suburbs and so many new synagogues have been built but the United Synagogue has not seen itself as a patron of Jewish art and architecture. Money has been found to re-build extremely expensive synagogues in Central London on valuable sites: the Marble Arch in Great Cumberland Place, the Central in Great Portland Street and the St. John's Wood, Grove End Road. The best that can be said of these undistinguished buildings is that they are comfortable and the designs are eclectic. Architecturally, they add little that is distinctive or Jewish to London's synagogues.

That it need not be so is clear from the contrast with the picture in the USA. Modern American synagogues have been built in a variety of styles and both Orthodox and non-Orthodox congregations have encouraged originality in architecture and decorative art. Eminent Jewish and non-Jewish architects have designed bold new temples: Eric Mendelsohn is responsible for original buildings in Cleveland, Ohio (Park Synagogue) and in St. Louis (B'nai Emoonah Synagogue, with its amazing parabolic roof-structure); Frank Lloyd Wright designed the Beth Shalom in Pennsylvania and Sydney Eisenstadt was commissioned to build the Mount Sinai Temple at El Paso, Texas. Jews in America have generously and imaginatively called upon a great range of artists and craftsmen to add to the meaning and visual pleasure of being in a synagogue. The work of sculptors, painters, fabric designers, graphic artists and metal craftsmen have been liberally used and displayed.

Where then are the Jewish architects and artists who might have added to the beauty and distinctiveness of the modern London synagogue? There is not really a shortage of talented Jewish artists and architects, so one

must attribute the failure to the patrons – not only the United Synagogue but all the Anglo-Jewish Synagogue Movements, the Ministers and congregations. Perhaps the Orthodox authorities in Britain are still inhibited by the old prohibition on 'representational art' – no 'graven images in the synagogue'? It seems unlikely. There are plenty of stained-glass windows in our synagogues with a variety of images of animals, plants and signs of the Zodiac. And the further back one goes in synagogue history, the more decoration one finds: the first Sephardi synagogue in Creechurch Lane had painted figures of Moses and Aaron, and recent archaeological discoveries in Israel have revealed ancient synagogues with elaborate mosaics depicting the sacrifice of Isaac (at the synagogue at Bet Alfa, the Valley of Jezreel) and a wealth of other images of men, women and animals.

No survey of contemporary trends in synagogue building and the congregations for whom they were designed, should overlook the revival of ultra-Orthodoxy. In spite of their relatively small numbers, the Chasidim have begun to play an important role in Jewish attitudes, if only because many ordinary Orthodox Anglo-Jews regard them with some awe as the standard-bearers of traditional Judaism. The Chasidim are not, however, much interested in synagogues as buildings. Like the Puritans, they are opposed to beautiful temples which distract the truly religious from worship. The Chasidim essentially prefer the *shtiebl* – the simple back room of the Rabbi's home. The synagogues they have built, therefore, have tended to be small and modern in a 'functional' style. In some cases they have preferred to convert old houses in Stamford Hill or simple prefabricated buildings (such as the Hampstead Adath Yisroel). So far, these ultra-Orthodox congregations have not contributed anything distinctive to London's synagogue architecture. It is quite possible that they will encourage the building of modest synagogues as an integral part of the communal requirements of their very active congregations. A real need certainly exists for modern synagogues that meet the multiple functions of the ancient synagogue: a suitable place to meet and be sociable, a place for teaching and the study of Judaism and a house of worship. There are signs that Jewish architects are being commissioned at last to design Community Centres incorporating an auditorium for services that can expand or diminish as required. (The new synagogue at Pinner designed by Alex Flinder is a successful example of the communal concept.)

There are, then, some hopeful signs, especially in the

outer suburbs of London. Lavish expenditure on big synagogues in the West End or in St. John's Wood has too often produced pretentious opulence unsuited to either Orthodox or Progressive congregations in our time. Limited budgets, on the other hand, have sometimes challenged the architect to produce satisfying contemporary buildings: the Kingsbury Synagogue designed by David Stern is unusual for London (the plan is based on the Star of David) and very satisfying; the Woodford Synagogue (1954) designed by Harold Weinrach, is fresh in concept and beautifully set in its own garden.

Architecture generally in the last 40 years has contributed little to the beauty of London. It is hard to think of many outstandingly successful modern buildings, whether for public or private purposes. Good synagogue building cannot spring out of an architectural desert: it needs a settled society, and enlightened patronage. There is unfortunately both a British and an Anglo-Jewish philistinism which together have been a negative influence in matters of synagogue design and decoration. There are at least official bodies that advise on church design and the care of churches. The United Synagogue in the last 50 years has shown much more concern about finance than about aesthetic considerations. And we cannot blame the Synagogue authorities alone; neither the Rabbis nor their congregations seem much interested either.

Anglo-Jewry has changed greatly in the last generation and the confusion in our society generally is the background to the problems in art and architecture. Paradoxically, British Jews are both more confident of their place in British society and more unsure of their Jewish identity. The establishment of the State of Israel has had its impact on Jews in England and changed their self-awareness. Since the 1970s Orthodox Jews have begun to wear their *yarmulkas* in the street, and Jews in London and elsewhere have lost their fear of arousing anti-semitism in their non-Jewish neighbours by being openly Jewish. Yet at the same time, the Anglo-Jew, like many American Jews, is troubled by the continuing argument in Israel and beyond about 'Who is a Jew?' Undoubtedly we are experiencing a breakdown in the consensus about Jewishness. The diversity of synagogues, movements and 'sects' is as obvious in London as in Israel or in the USA. Of course, there have always been differences in Jewish beliefs and practices but the gulfs seemed bridgeable in the past. A Jew used to be able to go into a synagogue in New York, Hong Kong or London and feel himself accepted and 'at home'. It is no longer so, and the polarising forces are so strong that Jewish identity is only unquestioned among extremists. In such a society, we could get an exciting variety of architectural solutions to the demands of our diverse congregations. We may also get very bland buildings that try to please everyone and satisfy no-one in particular.

Whatever the future holds for London's synagogues, it would be irresponsible to neglect what we have. Much has been lost and destroyed in the older districts of the City and in the East End. However much we need new designs and new buildings, this should not mean neglecting the past and ignoring the threat to historic synagogues as they are abandoned. It is shameful how little has been recorded or photographed of late Georgian or early nineteenth-century synagogues. (The London Museum of Jewish Life – formerly the Jewish East End Museum – had difficulty recently in mounting an exhibition of East End synagogues even with the help of the Federation and the generosity of individuals.) Few guide-books even mention the synagogues of London; non-Jews are not aware that London has such a range of temples, and most Jewish Londoners do not care very much about the synagogues of other Jews.

There is, however, a re-awakening of interest in things Jewish and in Anglo-Jewish history – even the recent establishment of new London Jewish museums is a hopeful sign. This book has tried to show the wealth and diversity of London's synagogues and that there is a heritage to be preserved. If we know what we have, there is a better chance that we may come to value it.

Notes

1. A description of the Spitalfields Great Synagogue.
2. United Synagogue Committee.
3. Section on the East End Synagogue.
4. The Central, the New West End, the West End Great, the Western, the Marble Arch, the West London and the West Central.

Notes on Sources

Acknowledgement is made to the following:

Edward Jamilly, 'Synagogue Art and Architecture' in Salmond S. Levin (ed.) *A Century of Anglo-Jewish Life* (London: United Synagogues, 1971).
Judy Glasman, 'Architecture and Anglicisation: London Synagogue Building, 1870–1900' *The Jewish Quarterly*, Vol.34, No.2, 1987.

Appendix 1

The Architects

Hyman Henry Collins
London:
    Bryanston Street Sephardic, 1862–63
    Borough New, 1867
    Barnsbury, 1868
    Repaired the Western, 1857, and Abbey Road, 1880

Henry David Davis and Barrow Emanuel
London:
    Upper Berkeley Street, 1867–70
    Stepney Green, 1876
    Lauderdale Road, 1896

John Davies
London:
    The New Synagogue, Great St Helen's, Bishopsgate, 1837

C.J. Epril (with Hersh)
London:
    Walm Lane, Willesden, 1930

Alex Flinder
Pinner:
    1979–82

Delissa Joseph
(Nephew of N.S. Joseph)
London:
    Hammersmith, 1890
    South Hackney, 1897
    Finsbury Park, 1901
    New Cross, 1904
Cardiff:
    1897
Manchester:
    Withington

Ernest M. Joseph
London:
    The New Synagogue, Egerton Road, 1915

Nathan Solomon Joseph
London:
    Bayswater, 1862–64 (with associates)
    Central, 1866–70
    New West End, 1878–79
    Dalston, 1885

Belfast:
    Victoria Street, 1870

Eric Lyons
London:
    Belsize Square, 1950s

David Mocatta
London:
    Bruton Street (Reform), 1842
    Margaret Street, W1, 1849
Ramsgate:
    1831–33

Edward Salomons
London:
    Bayswater (with N.S. Joseph), 1862–63
Manchester:
    Cheetham Hill, 1872–74

Derek Sharp
London:
    Amhurst Park and
Hove:
    Reform, 1960

Digby L. Solomon
London:
    Golders Green, 1921

Lewis Solomon
London:
    Old Castle Street, W1, 1872
    Spital Square, 1886
    Bethnal Green, 1891
    New Hambro', 1899
    Stoke Newington, 1903

David Stern (& Partners)
London:
    Kingsbury, 1970

Harald Weinreich
London:
    Woodford, 1954

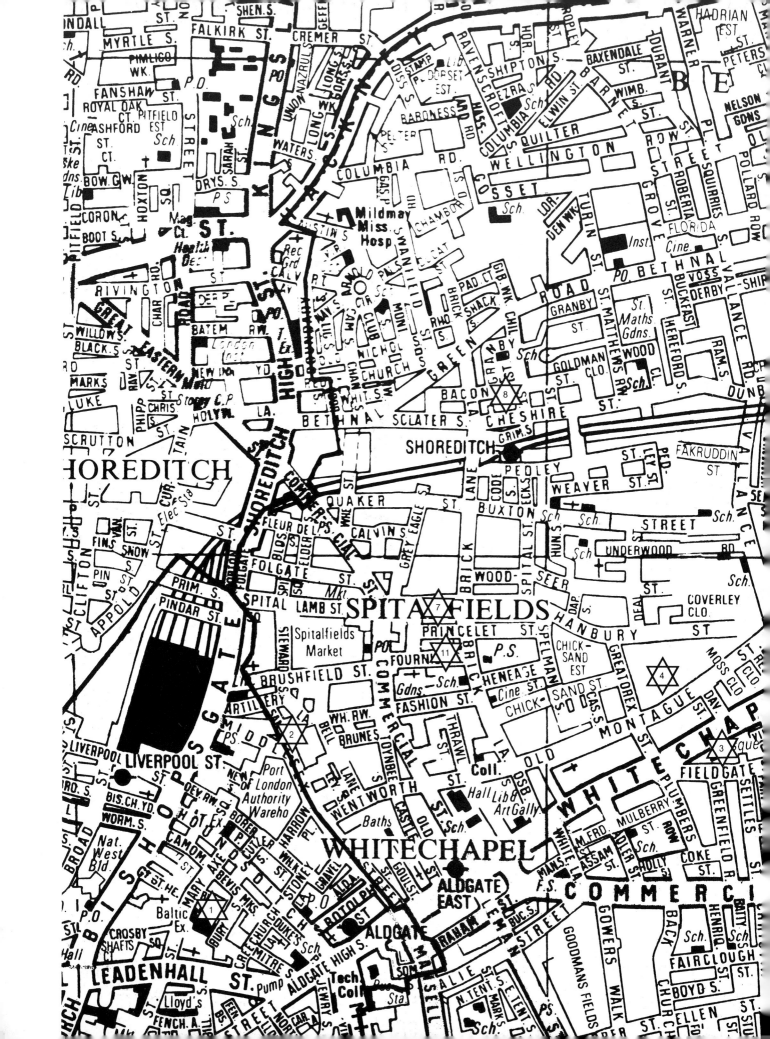

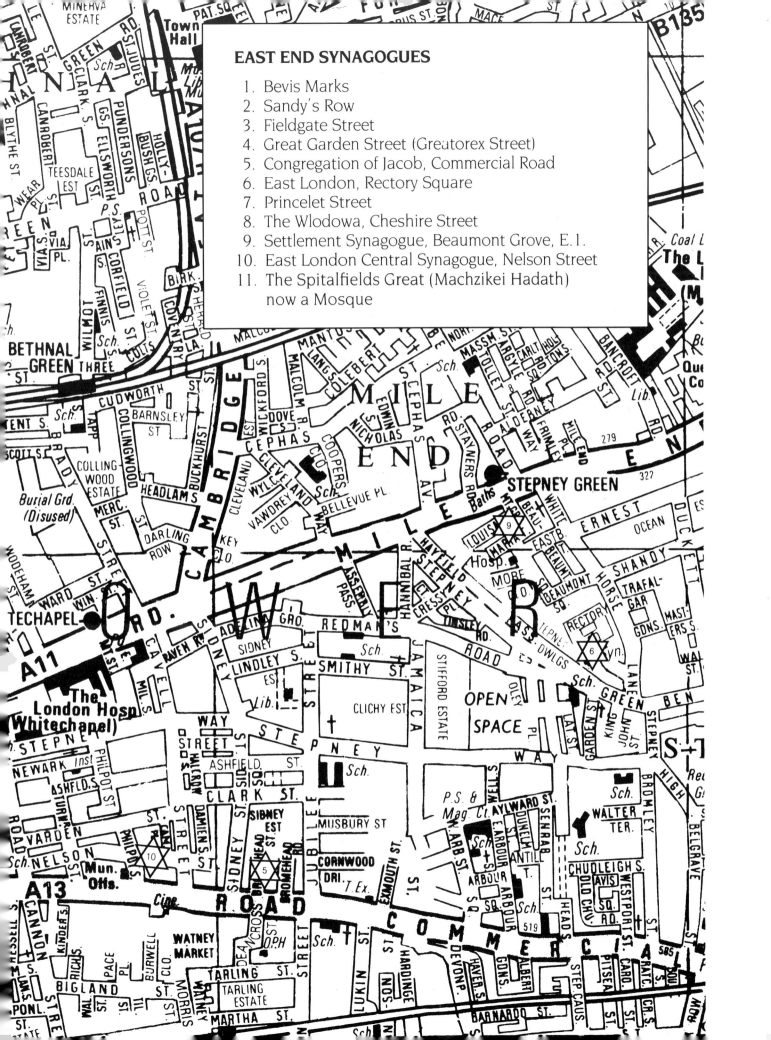

EAST END SYNAGOGUES

1. Bevis Marks
2. Sandy's Row
3. Fieldgate Street
4. Great Garden Street (Greatorex Street)
5. Congregation of Jacob, Commercial Road
6. East London, Rectory Square
7. Princelet Street
8. The Wlodowa, Cheshire Street
9. Settlement Synagogue, Beaumont Grove, E.1.
10. East London Central Synagogue, Nelson Street
11. The Spitalfields Great (Machzikei Hadath)
    now a Mosque

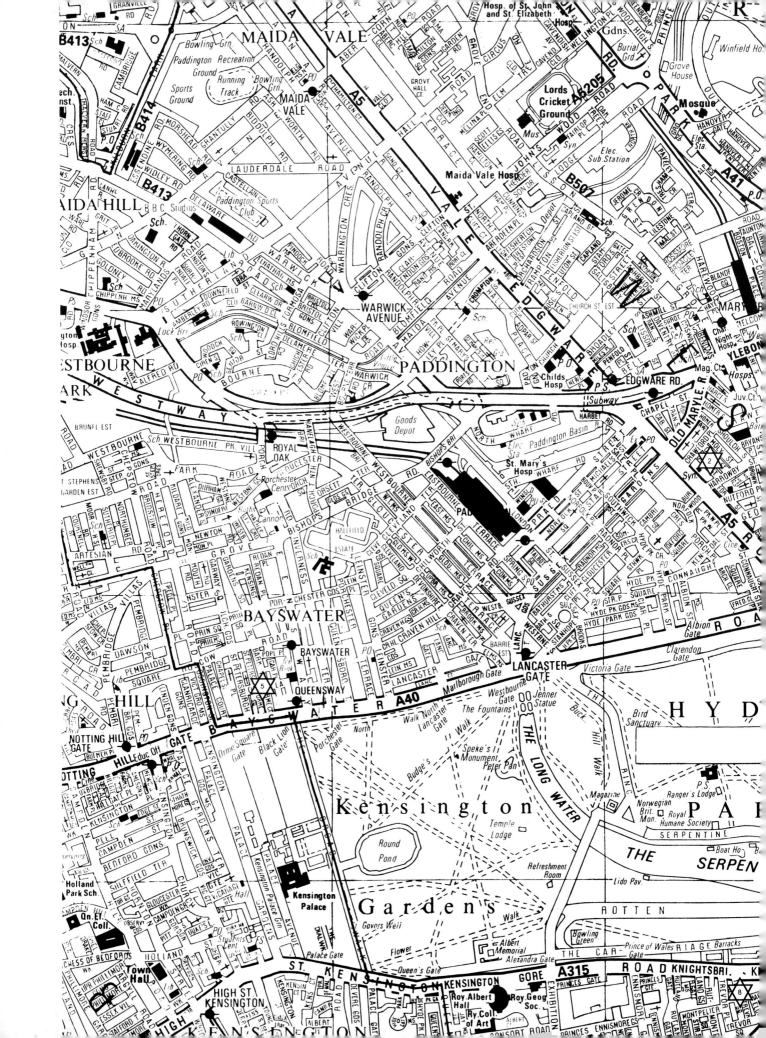

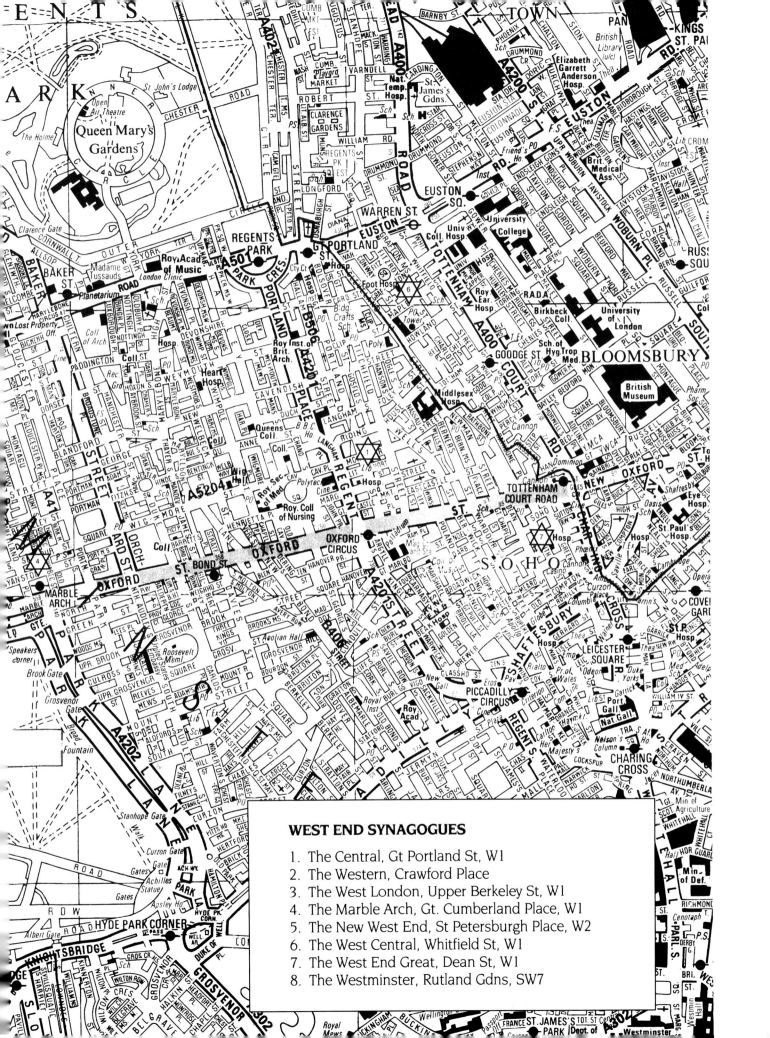

WEST END SYNAGOGUES

1. The Central, Gt Portland St, W1
2. The Western, Crawford Place
3. The West London, Upper Berkeley St, W1
4. The Marble Arch, Gt. Cumberland Place, W1
5. The New West End, St Petersburgh Place, W2
6. The West Central, Whitfield St, W1
7. The West End Great, Dean St, W1
8. The Westminster, Rutland Gdns, SW7

Appendix 3

Directory of Synagogues of Greater London

The synagogues are listed under synagogue movements or as independent congregations. The area covered includes Greater London and the outer suburbs.

Sephardi
Spanish and Portuguese
Congregations

Head Office: 2 Ashworth Road, W9

Bevis Marks: St Mary Axe, EC3
Lauderdale Road: Maida Vale, W9
Holland Park Synagogue: 8 St James's Gardens, W11
Wembley: 46 Forty Avenue, Wembley, Middlesex
Aden Jews' Congregation: 117 Clapton Common, E5
Eastern Jewry Community: Station Hall, Newbury Park, Ilford, Essex
Jacob Benjamin Elias (Gan Eden) Synagogue: 140 Stamford Hill, N16
Ilford Congregation (Ohel David): Newbury Park Station, Ilford, Essex
Neveh Shalom Community (David Ishag Synagogue): 352–354 Preston Road, Harrow, Middlesex
Ohel David Eastern Synagogue: Lincoln Institute, Broadwalk Lane, Golders Green, NW11
Persian Hebrew Congregational: 5a East Bank, N16

Ashkenazi
United Synagogue

Chief Rabbinate and Head Office: Woburn House, Upper Woburn Place, WC1

Barking and Becontree: 200 Becontree Avenue, Dagenham, Essex
Barnet: Eversleigh Road, New Barnet, Herts.
Belmont: 101 Vernon Drive, Stanmore, Middlesex
Borehamwood, Elstree and Radlett: Croxdale Road, Borehamwood, Herts.
Bushey and District: Sparrows Herne, Bushey Heath, Herts.
Catford and Bromley: 6 Crantock Road, Catford, SE6

Central: Great Portland Street, W1
Chelsea: Smith Terrace, Smith Street, SW3
Chigwell and Hainault: Limes Farm Avenue, Chigwell, Essex
Cockfosters and North Southgate: Old Farm Avenue, N14
Cricklewood: 131 Walm Lane, NW2
Dollis Hill: Parkside, Dollis Hill Lane, NW2
Ealing: 15 Grange Road, W5
East Ham and Manor Park: 28 Carlyle Road, E12
East London: 52 Rectory Square, Stepney Green, E1
Edgware: Edgware Way, Edgware, Middlesex.
Edmonton and Tottenham: 41 Lansdowne Road, N17
Elm Park: 75 Woburn Avenue, Hornchurch, Essex
Enfield and Winchmore Hill: 53 Wellington Road, Bush Hill Park, Enfield, Middlesex
Finchley: Kinloss Gardens, N3
Finsbury Park: Green Lanes, N4
Golders Green: 41 Dunstan Road, NW11
Hackney: Brenthouse Road, E9
Hammersmith and West Kensington: 71 Brook Green, W6
Hampstead: 1 Dennington Park Road, NW6
Hampstead Garden Suburb: Norrice Lea, N2
Harold Hill: Trowbridge Road, Harold Hill, Essex
Hendon: Raleigh Close, NW4.
Highams Park and Chingford: 74 Marlborough Road, E4
Highgate: Grimshaw Close, North Road, N6
Hounslow: 98 Staines Road, Hounslow, Middlesex
Ilford: 24 Beehive Lane, Ilford, Essex
Kenton: Shaftesbury Avenue, Kenton, Middlesex
Kingsbury: Kingsbury Green, NW9
Kingston and Surbiton: 33–35 Uxbridge Road, Kingston, Surrey
Marble Arch: 32 Great Cumberland Place, W1
Mill Hill: Brockenhurst Gardens, Mill Hill, NW7
Muswell Hill: 31 Tetherdown, N10
New: Egerton Road, N16
Newbury Park: 23 Wessex Close, Suffolk Road, Newbury Park, Essex
New West End: St Petersburgh Place, W2
Palmers Green and Southgate: Brownlow Road, N11
Pinner: 1 Cecil Park, Pinner, Middlesex
Richmond: Field House, Friars Stile Road, Twickenham, Middlesex
Romford: 25 Eastern Road, Romford, Essex

Ruislip: Shenley Avenue, Ruislip Manor, Middlesex
St John's Wood: 37–41 Grove End Road, NW8
South Hampstead: Eton Road, NW3
South London: 45 Leigham Court Road, SW16
South Tottenham: 11 Crowland Road, N15
South-West London: 104 Bolingbroke Gardens, SW11
Staines: Westbrook Road, South Street, Staines, Middlesex
Stanmore and Canons Park: London Road, Stanmore, Middlesex
Sutton: 14 Cedar Road, Sutton, Surrey
Wanstead and Woodford: 20 Churchfields, E18
Wembley: Forty Avenue, Wembley, Middlesex
West Ham and Upton Park: 93–95 Earlham Grove, E7
Willesden and Brondesbury: 143–145 Brondesbury Park, NW2
Woodside Park: Woodside Hall, Woodside Park Road, N12

The Federation of Synagogues

Head Office: 9–11 Greatorex Street, E1

Ahavath Shalom: Clifford Way, Neasden, NW10
Croydon and District: 30 Elmwood Road, Croydon, Surrey
Congregation of Jacob: 351–353 Commercial Road, E1
East London Central: 30–40 Nelson Street, E1
Fieldgate Street Great: 41 Fieldgate Street, E1
Finchley Central: Redbourne Avenue, N3
Great Garden Street: 7 Greatorex Street, E1
Greenford: 39–45 Oldfield Lane, Greenford, Middlesex
Ilford Federation: 16 Coventry Road, Ilford, Essex
Leytonstone and Wanstead: 2 Fillebrook Road, E11
Loughton, Chigwell and District: Bordens Lane, Loughton, Essex
New Wimbledon and Putney District: Greenfield House, Inner Park Road, SW19
Notting Hill: 206–208 Kensington Park Road, W11
Sha'are Shomayim (Clapton Federation Synagogue): 47 Lea Bridge Road, E5
Ohel Jacob Beth Hamedrash: Ilford, Essex
Shomrei-Hadath: 527a Finchley Road, NW3
Sinai: 54 Woodstock Avenue, NW11
Springfield: 202 Upper Clapton Road, E5
Stamford Hill Beth Hamedrash: 50 Clapton Common, E5
Tottenham Hebrew Congregation: 366 High Road, N17
West Hackney: 233a Amhurst Road, E8
Woolwich and District: Anglesea Road, Woolwich, SE8
Yavneh: 25 Ainsworth Road, E9
Yeshurun: Fernhurst Gardens, Edgware, Middlesex

Union of Orthodox Hebrew Congregations

Head Office: 40 Queen Elizabeth's Walk, N16

Adath Yisroel: 40 Queen Elizabeth's Walk, N16
Adath Yisroel Tottenham Beth Hamedrash: 55–57 Ravensdale Road, N16
Ahavat Israel Synagogue D'Chasidey Viznitz: 89 Stamford Hill, N16

Beth Abraham: 46 The Ridgeway, NW11
Beth Chodosh: 51 Queen Elizabeth's Walk, N16
Beth Hamedrash: 137 Golders Green Road, NW11
Beth Hamedrash Beis Nadvorna: 45 Darenth Road, N16
Beth Hamedrash D'Chasidey Belz: 99 Bethune Road, N16
Beth Hamedrash D'Chasidey Belz: 96 Clapton Common, E5
Beth Hamedrash D'Chasidey Gur: 2 Lampard Grove, N16
Beth Hamedrash D'Chasidey Ryzin: 33 Paget Road, N16
Beth Hamedrash D'Chasidey Square: 22 Dunsmure Road, N16
Beth Hamedrash D'Chasidey Sanz-Klausenburg: 42 Craven Walk, N16
Beth Hamedrash Divrei Chaim: 71 Bridge Lane, NW11
Beth Hamedrash Hendon: 3 The Approach, NW4 2HU
Beth Hamedrash Ohel Naphtoli: Egerton Road, N16
Beth Hamedrash Imrey Chaim D'Chassidey Vishnitz-Monsey: 121 Clapton Common, E5
Beth Hamedrash Ahel Shmuel Sholem: 37 Craven Walk, N16
Beth Hamedrash of the Agudah Youth Movement: 69 Lordship Road, N16
Beth Hamedrash Torah Etz Chayim: 69 Lordship Road, N16
Beth Hamedrash Torah Chaim Liege: 145 Upper Clapton Road, E5
Beth Hamedrash Yetiv Lev: 86 Cazenove Road, N16
Beth Israel (Trisker): 146 Osbaldeston Road, N16
Beth Shmuel: 171 Golders Green Road, NW11
Beth Sholom: 27 St Kilda's Road, N16
Beth Talmud Centre: 78 Cazenove Road, N16
Beth Yisochor Dov Beth Hamedrash: 4 Highfield Avenue, NW11
Birkath Yehuda (Halaser) Beth Hamedrath: 47 Moundfield Road, N16
Bridge Lane Beth Hamedrath: 44 Bridge Lane, NW11
Finchley Road: 4 Helenslea Avenue, NW11
Frumkins Beth Hamedrath: 10a Woodberry Down, N4
Garden Suburb Beth Hamedrath: Jacob Gordon House, 5 The Bishop's Avenue, N2
Hampstead Adath Yisroel Congregation: 10a Cranfield Gardens, NW6
Hendon Adath Yisroel: 11 Brent Street, NW4
Kehillath Chasidim: 85 Cazenove Road, N16
Knightland Road Synagogue of the Law of Truth Tamudical College: 50 Knightland Road, E5
Lubavitch: 107–115 Stamford Hill, N16
Mesifta: 82–84 Cazenove Road, N16
North Hendon Adath: Holders Hill Road, NW4
Ohel Israel (Skoler): 11 Brent Street, NW4
Stanislowa Beth Hamedrath: 93 Lordship Park, N16
Yeshiva Horomoh Beth Hamedrath: 100 Fairholt Road, N16
Yeshuath Chaim: 45 Heathland Road, N16
Yesodey Hatorah: 2–4 Amhurst Park, N16

Independent Synagogues

Belsize Square: 51 Belsize Square, NW3
Commercial Road Talmud Torah (formerly at Christian Street, E1): 153 Stamford Hill, N16
Edgware Adath Yisroel: 261 Hale Lane, Edgware, Middlesex
Golders Green Beth Hamedrash Congregation: The Riding, Golders Green Road, NW11
Machzikei Hadath (affiliated to the Federation): 3 Highfield Road, NW11
Persian Hebrew Congregation: East Bank, N16
Sandy's Row: 4a Sandy's Row, Middlesex Street, E1
Walford Road: 99 Walford Road, Stoke Newington N16
Waltham Forest: 140 Boundary Road, E17
West End Great: 21 Dean Street, W1
Western Marble Arch: 32 Great Cumberland Place, W1
Westminster: Rutland Gardens, Knightsbridge, SW7

Masorti Synagogues

Administrative Office: 33 Abbey Road, NW8

Edgware Masorti: Brady Maccabi Centre, 4 Manor Park Crescent, Edgware, Middlesex
New Essex Masorti Congregation: 3 Beechcroft Road, South Woodford, E18
New London: 33 Abbey Road, St John's Wood, NW8
New North London: The Manor House, 80 East End Road, N3
South-West London Masorti: Tel: 081 946 9718/ 081 876 8977

Reform Synagogues

Headquarters: The Manor House, 80 East End Road, N3

Bromley and District: 28 Highland Road, Bromley, Kent
Buckhurst Hill: 1a Brook Road, Loughton, Essex
Edgware and District: 118 Stonegrove, Edgware, Middlesex
Finchley: Fallowcourt Avenue, N12
Hampstead Reform Jewish Community: 73 Leverton Street, NW5
Hendon: Danescroft Avenue, NW4
Kol Chai-Hatch End Jewish Community: 40 Holmdene Avenue, Harrow, Middlesex
Middlesex New: 39 Bessborough Road, Harrow, Middlesex
Mill Hill: 10 Derwent Avenue, NW7
North-Western: Alyth Gardens, Finchley Road, NW11
North-West Surrey: Horvath Close, Rosslyn Park, Oatlands Drive, Weybridge, Surrey
Radlett and Bushey: 118 Watling Street, Radlett, Herts.
Settlement Synagogue: 2–8 Beaumont Grove, E1
Southgate and District: 45 High Street, N14
South-West Essex: Oaks Lane, Newbury Park, Essex
West London: 34 Upper Berkeley Street, W1
Wimbledon and District: 44–46 Worple Road, SW19

Liberal Synagogues

Headquarters of Union of Liberal and Progressive Synagogues: 109 Whitfield Street, W1

Barkingside Progressive: 129 Perryman's Farm Road, Barkingside, Ilford, Essex
Ealing Liberal: Lynton Avenue, Drayton Green, W13
Finchley Progressive: 54a Hutton Grove, N12
Harrow and Wembley: 326 Preston Road, Harrow, Middlesex
Hertsmere Progressive: High Street, Elstree, Herts
Kingston Liberal: Rushett Road, Long Ditton, Surbiton, Surrey
Liberal Jewish: 28 St John's Wood Road, NW8
North London Progressive: 100 Amhurst Park, N16
Northwood and Pinner: Oaklands Gate, Green Lane, Northwood, Middlesex
Settlement Synagogue (also listed under Reform Synagogues): Beaumont Grove, E1
Southgate Progressive: 75 Chase Road, N14
South London Liberal: Prentis Road, Streatham, SW16
West Central: 109–113 Whitfield Street, W1
Woodford and District Liberal: Marlborough Road, George Lane, E18

Glossary

almemar: the Sephardic name of the platform in the synagogue on which the reader's table is placed (see *bimah*).

amidah: prayer recited in the synagogue while standing.

Aron Ha-kodesh: The Ark or place in the synagogue in which the Scrolls of the Law are kept. *Aron ha-kodesh* is the Hebrew name used by the Ashkenazim; it is called *heikhal* by the Sephardim.

ascama (plural *ascamot*): a law of the Sephardic congregation.

Ashkenazi: originally the term applied to describe the Jews of medieval Germany or their descendants. Generally the Ashkenazim are Jews of Eastern European origin whose ritual is different from the Sephardim.

bar mitzvah: literally 'son of the commandment' – the ceremony of bar mitzvah marks the initiation of a 13-year-old boy into the Jewish community as an adult man with responsibility and obligations to perform the commandments and take part in communal prayers.

bat mizvah or *Chayil*: the ceremony in the synagogue for a girl aged 12 years and a day who takes on the obligations to fulfil the religious commandments applicable to an adult woman.

beth din: literally, 'house of judgement' or Jewish Law Court conducted by the rabbinical authorities.

beth Haknesset: the original Hebrew name of the synagogue – literally, the house of assembly or communal meeting place.

beth hamidrash: literally, 'house of study' – a school for rabbinic study; in former times it was independent or attached to the synagogue.

bimah: the platform on which the reader's desk is placed for the reading of the Torah. Traditionally in the centre of the synagogue, in recent times it is usually in front of the Ark. (Also called *almemar* or *tevah* by the Sephardim.)

Chanukah (Hanukah): the festival celebrated for eight days beginning on 25th Kislev commemorating the Hasmonean victory. Also called the Feast of Lights.

Chasidim (Hasidim): originally the followers of an eighteenth-century religious movement founded by Israel Baal Shem Tov. The term is now used loosely to mean the adherents of extremely Orthodox movements who follow their own rabbis.

Chazan: the cantor, who leads the prayers by singing or chanting.

cheder: Hebrew school, or classroom where Hebrew is taught.

chevra (plural *chevrot*): literally a society or voluntary association. The term came to mean the small synagogues which developed from the 'friendly societies' of poor, working-class Jews, the Eastern European immigrants to London in the late nineteenth and early twentieth centuries.

chupa: the canopy used at the wedding ceremony in the synagogue.

davan: Yiddish, meaning 'pray'.

dayan: a member (a judge) of a rabbinical court.

duchan: literally, a 'platform' from which to recite the priestly benedictions.

Haham: the title of the Chief Rabbi of the Sephardi community.

herem: an excommunication or ban.

kaddish: an Aramaic word meaning 'holy'; used to name the prayer for mourners recited during the synagogue service.

kashrut: the rules and laws governing diet and the preparation of food.

kehilla (plural *kehillot*): community.

kiddush: means 'sanctification'. The name of the prayer recited at the beginning of the Sabbath (Friday evening) and on Holy days.

Ladino: a dialect spoken by Jews of Spanish origin – a mixture of medieval Castilian, Hebrew, Greek and Turkish.

menorah: the candelabrum, originally with seven branches, but in modern times with eight or nine. The *menorah* has become the emblem of Israel.

minyan: a quorum of ten adult male Jews – the minimum required for communal prayer.

ner tamid: 'the eternal lamp'. It is customary to hang a permanently illuminated lamp in front of the Ark in the synagogue.

payess: sideburn-locks worn by ultra-Orthodox Jewish men and boys.

Rosh Ha-Shanah: 1st and 2nd of Tishri (September–October): the New Year festival observed for two days.

schnorrer: Yiddish (from the German 'schnorren' = to beg) for a beggar but used pejoratively to mean a shrewd professional mendicant.

sedra: weekly readings from the Torah.

Sefer (pl. *Sifrei*) *Torah*: the hand-written Scroll of the Pentateuch used for reading publicly in the synagogue; kept in the Ark when not in use.

Sephardi (plural Sephardim): Jews of Spanish and Portuguese origin and their descendants; now used loosely for Jews from Oriental countries.

Shabbat: the Sabbath – the day of rest observed from sunset on Friday to Saturday evening.

shammas: the synagogue official – similar to a church beadle.

sheitel: the wig traditionally worn after marriage by Orthodox Ashkenazi women.

shivah: the seven days of mourning beginning immediately after the funeral when the family 'sit shivah' in the home of the dead relative.

shmutta (Yiddish): a rag or a piece of rubbishy material.

shtetl: Yiddish term denoting a small town or village – especially the home of the communities of Eastern Europe before 1914.

shtiebl (plural *shtieblach*: (Yiddish) the prayer room or small one-roomed synagogue of the Hasidim.

shtreimel: a fur-trimmed hat, worn by the Chasidim, especially from Poland or Galicia.

shul: the Yiddish word for the synagogue.

Simchat Torah: literally 'rejoicing of the Law': the festival or Holy Day marking the completion of the annual cycle of readings of the Pentateuch in the synagogue.

snoga: the old Sephardic name for the synagogue.

Sukkah: a 'tabernacle' – leaf-covered temporary structure erected in the open air in which meals are taken during the autumn festival of Sukkoth.

talluth (or *tallit*): a prayer shawl, with fringes at each corner, worn by male worshippers at most services in the synagogue.

Talmud: apart from the Bible, the most important body of Jewish law.

Talmud Torah: ('Study of the Torah') a school devoted to Jewish religious learning.

yarmulka: (Yiddish) a skull-cap.

yeshiva: (Yiddish) a school for the advanced study of the Talmud.

Yom Kippur: the Day of Atonement – the most solemn day of fasting and prayer of the Jewish year.

Bibliography

Adler, Michael, *The History of the Hammersmith Synagogue* (London: Edward Goldston, 1950).

Apple, Raymond, *The Hampstead Synagogue, 1892–1967* (London: Vallentine, Mitchell, 1967).

Barnett, A., *The Western Synagogue Through Two Centuries* (London: Vallentine, Mitchell, 1961).

Barnett, R.D. and Levy, A., *The Bevis Marks Synagogue* (London: Society of Heshaim, 1975).

Bermant, Chaim, *Troubled Eden* (London: Vallentine, Mitchell, 1969).

Bernstein, M., *Stamford Hill and the Jews before 1915* (London: M.S.B. Publications, 1976).

Besant, Walter, *East London* (London: Chatto & Windus, 1909).

Diamond, A.S., *The Building of a Synagogue* (London: West London Synagogue, 1970).

Edgar, Rabbi Dr Leslie I., *In Memory of Lily Montagu* (Amsterdam: Polak & Van Gennep, 1967).

Finestein, I., 'Joseph F. Stern, 1865–1934: Aspects of a Gifted Anomaly' in A. Newman (ed.), *The Jewish East End 1840–1939* (London: The Jewish Historical Society of England, 1981).

Glasman, Judy, 'Architecture and Anglicisation', *The Jewish Quarterly*, Vol.34, No.2 (1987).

Homa, B., *Fortress in Anglo-Jewry. The Story of the Machzike Hadath* (London: Shapiro Vallentine, 1953).

Hyamson, A.M., *A History of the Jews in England* (London: Methuen, 1928).

Jamilly, Edward, 'Synagogue Art and Architecture', in Salmond S. Levin (ed.), *A Century of Anglo-Jewish Life* (London: United Synagogue, 1971).

Kadish, Sharman, Letter published in *The Jewish Chronicle*, 18 December 1987.

Kershen, Anne J. (ed.), *1840–1990 150 Years of Progressive Judaism in Britain* (London: Museum of Jewish Life, 1990).

Krinsky, Carol, *The Synagogues of Europe* (Cambridge, MA: The M.I.T. Press, 1985).

Levin, Salmond S. (ed.), *A Century of Anglo-Jewish Life* (London: United Synagogue, 1971).

Levy, A.B., *The 200-year-old New Synagogue* (London: New Synagogue, 1960).

Levy, Abraham, *The Synagogue at Lauderdale Road* (London: The Society of Heshaim, 1971).

Lipman, V.D., *Social History of the Jews in England, 1850–1950* (London: Watts & Co., 1954).

Mayhew, Henry, *London Labour and the London Poor* (ed. Peter Quennell; London: Bracken Books, 1984).

Newman, A., *The United Synagogue, 1870–1970* (London: Routledge & Kegan Paul, 1976).

Pepys, Samuel, *The Diary of Samuel Pepys* (London: J.M. Dent, 1906 ed.).

Pevsner, Nicholas, *The Buildings of England* (Harmondsworth: Penguin, 1957).

Phillips, Aga Somech and Simons, Hyman A., *The History of the Bayswater Synagogue* (London, 1963).

Potter, Beatrice, 'The Jews of London' in Charles Booth (ed.), *Life and Labour of the People* (London: Macmillan, 2nd ed. 1892–97).

Roth, Cecil, *The Federation of Synagogues 1912–1937* (London: The Federation of Synagogues, 1937).

–, *History of the Great Synagogue* (London: Edward Goldston, 1950).

–, *The Rise of Provincial Jewry* (London: The Jewish Monthly, 1950).

–, *A History of the Jews in England* (Oxford: Oxford University Press, 1964).

Shaffer, Ruth, *et al.*, *The Czech Memorial Scrolls Centre* (London: Scrolls Memorial Trust, 1988).

Shine, Rabbi Cyril I., *A History of the Central Synagogue* (London: The Central Synagogue, 1970).

Waterman, S. and Kosmin, B., *British Jewry in the Eighties* (London: Board of Deputies of British Jews, 1986).

Wigoder, G., *The Story of the Synagogue* (London: Weidenfeld & Nicolson, 1986).

Other sources

Acknowledgement is made to the *Jewish Chronicle* for a number of quotations referred to in the text (dates cited); to the *Jewish Year Book* (London: *Jewish Chronicle* Publications, 1986–91); and to Jonathan A. Romain, *The Jews of England* (London: The Michael Goulston Foundation in association with *Jewish Chronicle* Publications, 1988).